VILLA BALBIANO

VILLA BALBIANO

ITALIAN OPULENCE ON LAKE COMO

TEXT RUBEN MODIGLIANI PHOTOGRAPHY BRUNO EHRS

ORIGINAL WATERCOLORS
ANDREW ZEGA AND BERND H. DAMS

Flammarion

"For miles along the shores, handsome country seats, surrounded by gardens and groves, sit fairly in the water, sometimes in nooks carved by Nature out of the vine-hung precipices, and with no ingress or egress save by boats. Some have great broad stone staircases leading down to the water, with heavy stone balustrades ornamented with statuary and fancifully adorned with creeping vines and bright-colored flowers—for all the world like a drop curtain in a theater."

Mark Twain, *The Innocents Abroad*, 1869.

PAGES 2-3 The visual axis of water and greenery leading to the front door and the corresponding vista on the other side through the garden and down to the lake dictate the measured proportions of Villa Balbiano and its harmonious landscape setting.
PAGE 4 Irises and water lilies embellish the pool at the front gate, designed by Enrico Vuilliomenet in the 1970s.
FACING PAGE The majestic wrought-iron entrance gate opens onto a seventeenth-century oval vestibule with a pool in the center.

CONTENTS

FACING PAGE Detail of the fresco in the Sala delle Colonne with a bust of Giacomo Gallio supported by two cherubs, painted in the seventeenth century by Giovan Paolo and Raffaele Recchi.

PREFACE

There are special places in the world where nature, history, and art meet and interweave. In Italy, a land shaped by millennia of human activity (from tilling the soil to building cities), these encounters are quite frequent, almost uninterrupted. It was not by chance that young and not-so-young aristocrats traveled the country up and down and back and forth as far back as the seventeenth century on their Grand Tour, the great journey of Europe that was a sort of rite of passage for the offspring of the well-to-do. The word "tourism" derives precisely from that, and Italy has always been intimately bound up in it. The first vision to greet those crossing the Alps from the north—the great majority—was the Italian lake district. Here the air was immediately sweeter, as a sumptuous panorama opened before their eyes. It was the same landscape that greeted the Longobards when they arrived over a thousand years earlier, in the sixth century, from what is now Germany, and settled in the region south of the Alps that would later bear their name: Lombardy. After leaving their homeland, where the Elbe River flows, and setting up camp on the banks of the Danube, the path of the Longobards brought them here, where they finally settled, happy to have found a generous and beautiful land. Before them there had been the Romans, and before the Romans the many local populations. It was already a region rich in history.

But let's jump ahead to the modern day. Satellite images reveal a region where the plain begins to rise and wrinkle into hills and mountains. There is an area marked by long tongues of water nestled among the peaks. Among the many bodies of water, three large ones stand out: from west to east they are Lake Maggiore, Lake Lugano, and Lake Como. The last has a very distinctive form, like a Greek lambda or a divining rod. There is a small cove on its western shore embracing a tiny island, the only one on the lake. It is slightly south of Bellagio, which adorns its promontory on the other side of the lake. Zooming in closer, there is a small town on the lakeshore so close to the island that

PAGES 10–11 Villa Balbiano differs from other historical villas on Lake Como for its sober Renaissance architecture and perfectly balanced proportions.
FACING PAGE Lake Como at dusk from Villa Balbiano.

"The lake is contained in a very large and very deep valley … around it are clustered, forming a sort of crown, splendid high mountain passes … the shores embellished by villas … surrounded by a perpetually green sash of olive groves."

Cassiodorus, *Variae epistolae*, c. 537 CE.

one could swim between them. The town is Ossuccio. It features a few houses and a Romanesque church and oratory. At its eastern edge, there is a luxurious garden leading down to an elegant, austere villa. This is Villa Balbiano. Its simple, stately form, without excessive decorative flourishes, is not a sight one often sees on these shores: the villas on Lake Como generally belong to later, more ornate periods. Villa Balbiano is one of the oldest, tracing its origins to the fifteenth century. It has stood through centuries and eras, tastes and fashions, fortune and misfortune. It has belonged to important families, it has been a place of culture and delight, and also, during less fortunate times, an industrial facility.

Each period has left some mark, some trace: a stuccowork series, a cycle of frescoes and mural paintings, a fountain in the garden. In the second half of the twentieth century, the villa—whose plan has been altered by the many events over its history—once again became a home, but it was only recently that the decision was made to restore it to the stately grandeur of its origins. Work on the villa and the gardens moved in two directions. On the one hand, restoration work was carried out based on painstaking historical research that revealed no small number of surprises, making it possible to rediscover long-forgotten decorations. On the other hand, elements of the modern world (technology, new functions, new ways of living in the home environment) were introduced with great discernment into this context of enormous historical significance. A new chapter has thus been opened in the life of this unique place. This volume documents it with magnificent photographs, while its chapters tell the story of a passion for beauty that began more than two thousand years ago and is now more vibrant than ever. Villa Balbiano, the incarnation of an absolute ideal of fine living, is one of its most excellent fruits. ◆

FACING PAGE Two stone eagles stand as sentinels on the railing at the edge of the garden, guarding the view over the lake.
PAGES 16–17 The villa in its lush garden. The Sacro Monte di Ossuccio devotional complex with the Sanctuary of the Madonna del Soccorso, a UNESCO World Heritage Site, can be seen in the left background.

I

TWENTY CENTURIES OF CONQUESTS

THE VILLA: PRESTIGE AND PLEASURE

Words can often tell us much about our distant past. For example, the word "villa." A leading Italian encyclopedia defines it as follows: "in modern construction terminology, a type of single-family dwelling marked by a certain degree of luxury, surrounded by a garden of varying size." It continues with a discussion reaching back into history, to ancient Rome. Indeed, as often found in the Italian language, many modern words come completely unaltered from Latin. The word originally signified both land owned by an individual and the residential and agricultural buildings associated with it. The context is thus the countryside, with the first villas being farmhouses. It was in the first century BCE that villas became synonymous with refined lifestyles dedicated to the pursuit of pleasure. The villa was a comfortable and aesthetically pleasing place, built in an attractive setting, where the owners could enjoy their leisure time and became an ideal dwelling type that began to appear in cities as a symbol of the owner's prestige. The villa was a place for relaxation and meditation, a blend of culture and nature, each expressed at the highest level.

According to archaeological evidence, in all probability, Rome developed its first exquisitely urban elements in the late seventh century BCE. It is estimated that by the middle of the following century, it could already boast at least thirty thousand inhabitants. Less than three centuries later, on the eve of the first Punic War (c. 270–241 BCE), with approximately 186,000 residents, Rome was one of the major metropolises in the western Mediterranean region, second in population only to Carthage. By the end of the next century (in the late republican period), however, Rome had become the world's most populous city.

Under Augustus (63 BCE–14 CE), Rome was home to some one million people. It reached its maximum extent during the Antonine period (mid-second century CE) with somewhere between 1.2 and 1.7 million residents crowded into forty-nine thousand buildings, most of them multi-story. It was an immense,

FACING PAGE Detail from the decorations in the dining room of Villa Balbiano painted by the Milanese artist Giuseppe Porro in 1778.

crowded, noisy city. Major public works were undertaken to address and resolve issues deriving from this high concentration of inhabitants. The groundwork was laid for an urban planning scheme that is still applied across the globe: high-density residential land use with high-rise buildings accommodating the greatest number of people on the least amount of land.

Given the lack of any convenient means of mass transportation at the time, there was a great need to organize the population within the smallest space possible. Thus the *insulae*, the housing for the common folk, grew higher and higher. The *domus*, on the other hand, generally inhabited by a single family and their servants, tended to extend horizontally. In the imperial period, such buildings reached the height of seven floors. They would not have met today's safety standards: fires and structural failures were not uncommon. These structures were generally

organized with shops, public offices, and *tabernae* (inns) on the ground floor and residences on the upper floors. The walls were made of unfired brick with wooden floors and window frames. Open flames were used for heat and lighting (stoves and lamps), representing a significant fire risk. Often, the second level was embellished with balconies, and it was Roman custom to decorate these, along with windows and roofs, with plants. Some neighboring *insulae* were connected above street level by arched structures crossing the street below and providing other rooms to rent out, or simply enlarging an existing dwelling. The first and second floors were the most prestigious and also the most practical: one needed to climb only one flight of stairs to reach them, which was a great advantage generally, and also

FACING PAGE A late nineteenth-century British etching of an imperial Roman villa.
ABOVE Félix Duban (1797–1870), *Un palais romain sous l'Empire* (A Roman Palace under the Empire), 1831. Musée Condé, Chantilly.

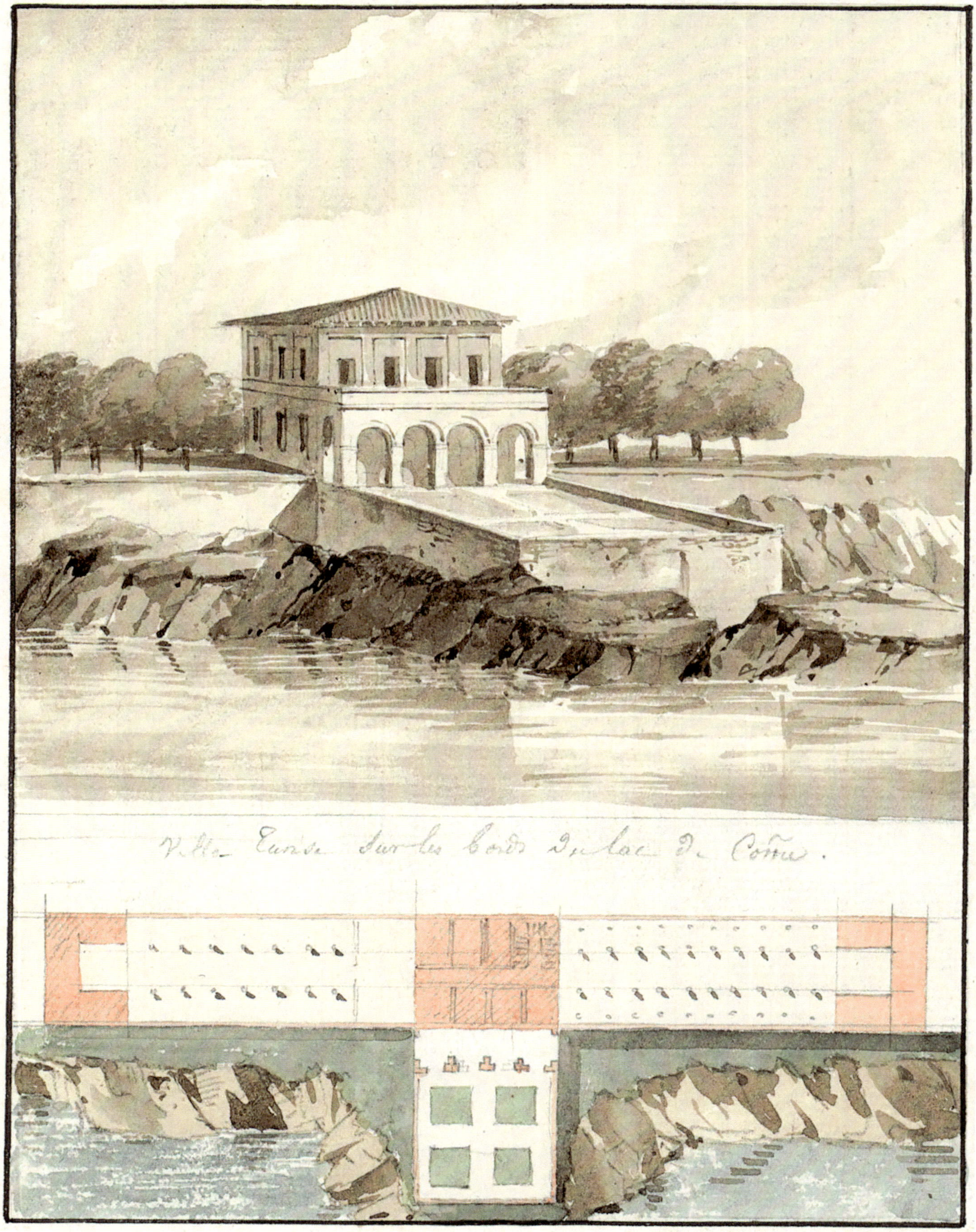

ABOVE Louis-Hippolyte Le Bas (1782–1867), *Villa Tunsi sur les bords du lac de Côme, vue et plan* (Villa Tunis on the Banks of Lake Como, Plan and Elevation), nineteenth century. École nationale supérieure des beaux-arts, Paris.
FACING PAGE Comacina Island is one of the most extraordinary archaeological sites in northern Italy with traces dating from the Roman epoch to the sixteenth century.

made evacuation much faster and safer in the event of fire. These spaces were thus destined for people with greater economic means. The higher the floor, the lower the social ranking.

The *domus*, on the other hand, was a completely different world. Generally laid out on a single level, such a building had no external windows or balconies, with all openings giving onto the central spaces. This provided protection from thieves, prying eyes, and noise. The only exception might have been a few small windows positioned high in the external walls. The entrance, consisting of a double door with bronze fittings, was generally located on one of the short sides of the structure. The *domus* was composed of rooms for the master of the house to receive guests

or do business, with other private spaces for family life. It was often built using prized materials. The back of the house included a kitchen or ornamental garden known as a *hortus*. This open-air space was often embellished with fountains and pools designed to create a harmonious setting to be enjoyed in all seasons. Particularly prestigious *domus* also featured a *bibliotheca* for books, a *pinacotheca* for works of art, and a *diaeta* for entertaining guests (from the Greek *diaita*, the etymon of "diet").

Rome was a crowded city. And it was also dangerous: the satirical poet Juvenal wrote that you would have to be crazy to go out at night in Rome without writing your last will and testament. Those who had the means found ways to get away from the city whenever possible—thus the origin of the vacation villa.

This new type of villa was located close to the city and stripped of any agricultural function. It was elegant and opulent, even more so than the *domus*, with porticoes and colonnades allowing the owners to enjoy the outdoors without venturing off their property. It had open-air and indoor dining rooms (*triclinia*) for the summer and winter, respectively, and rooms for an afternoon nap (*cubicula diurna*). There was also usually an office, a swimming pool, and a spa. Part of the villa's grounds was used as a kitchen garden and part as an ornamental garden with flowers, rare plants, fountains, waterworks, and statues.

The *horti* were another form of dwelling, similar in many ways to the vacation villas. They had large gardens and cultivated fields, but were built within the city walls at the edges of the city. These were also places of leisure and pleasure, where one could live in an isolated, peaceful setting. According to sources in Latin literature, Roman politician Lucullus (115–c. 57 BCE) pioneered this form of dwelling, building a sumptuous residence where he could receive his frequent guests. He planted woods and gardens with paths, vases, and finely worked wooden partitions. He installed floor mosaics in tiles or pebbles, and raised or inset fountains with colorful fish, an interplay of water jets, and waterworks. He sculpted hedges into various forms, and arranged exotic plants and trees to create various nuances and color combinations among brooks, scented grasses, vegetable gardens, and fields. Quite taken by the idea of living in the city while still immersed in nature, his guests began to imitate him. Thus the idea of living in a world as close to perfect as possible. And landscape design was very much a part of this, later giving birth to Italian and French gardens. The Roman villa, with its architecture and landscaping, provides the model for the villa as we understand it today. ◆

ABOVE Félix Auvray (1800–1833), *Villa romaine* (Roman Villa), 1826. Musée des Beaux-Arts, Valenciennes.
FACING PAGE Created in the image of a Roman villa, Balbiano offers outdoor spaces for relaxation with a view of the lake.

LAKE COMO AND ITS HISTORY

A very interesting letter fragment has survived from the Roman imperial period (which stretched from 31 BCE, the end of the thirteen-year civil war that marked the end of the republic, to the beginning of Diocletian's reign in 284 CE): "How stands Como, that favorite scene of yours and mine? What becomes of the pleasant villa, the ever-vernal portico?"

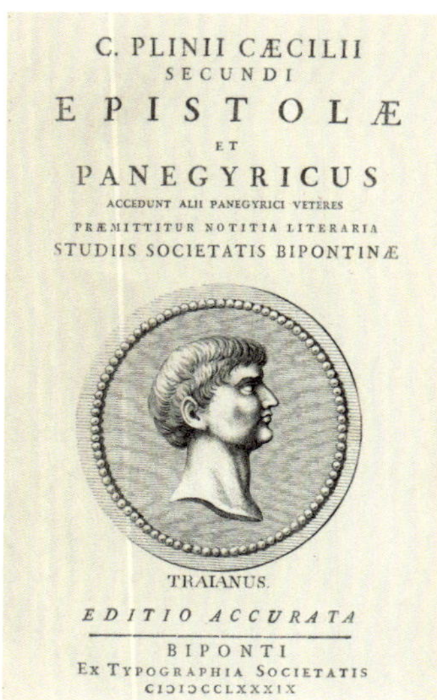
C. PLINII CÆCILII
SECUNDI
EPISTOLÆ
ET
PANEGYRICUS
ACCEDUNT ALII PANEGYRICI VETERES
PRÆMITTITUR NOTITIA LITERARIA
STUDIIS SOCIETATIS BIPONTINÆ
TRAIANUS.
EDITIO ACCURATA
BIPONTI
EX TYPOGRAPHIA SOCIETATIS
CIƆIƆCCLXXXIX

The letter was written by Pliny the Younger (c. 61–113 CE), author, military commander, and scientist, whose monumental thirty-seven-volume *Naturalis Historia* would remain a cornerstone of scientific knowledge well into the Renaissance. The letter is the first written source documenting the existence of a villa on Lake Como. And it was precisely in the imperial age that the lake region gained fame as a peaceful setting for intellectual leisure, a place that instills harmony of body and mind, where one may engage in recreation or indulge in literature and the pleasures of conversation. Its breath-taking panorama of steep mountainsides framing the three sinuous branches of Italy's deepest lake, and its unique climate, where the waters of the lake provide a mild Mediterranean oasis even in mid-winter, were certainly not lost on the Romans. For that matter, the region was already a cradle of civilization long before the Romans arrived. In the seventh century BCE, a civilization developed out of the union of the preexisting Ligurian peoples and the newly arriving Celts. We now refer to it as the Golasecca culture after the site of the first archaeological findings. It was concentrated in three principal population centers: the areas around Sesto Calende, Bellinzona, and, particularly, proto-urban Como. With the arrival of the Gauls from what is now France in the fourth century BCE, the Golasecca culture declined and died out. The transalpine Gauls occupied the Po River valley all the way to the Adriatic. Those who settled in what is now western Lombardy took the name of Insubres, while those settling further to the east were known as Cenomani. The latter, allies of the nearby Veneti, were often in conflict with the Insubres.

In the late third century BCE, the Romans began their conquest of the Po River valley, entering into conflict with the Insubres. In 196 BCE, the army of consul Marcus Claudius Marcellus defeated the inhabitants of Comum (Como) and took the city.

FACING PAGE Pliny the Younger's letters (*Epistolae*), written between 96 and 113 CE, are a precious source of information on the social and cultural life of his times.
ABOVE Illustration of the courtyard of villa Pliniana in *Voyage pittoresque et historique du nord de l'Italie* (Picturesque and Historical Voyage in the North of Italy) by Tønnes Christian Bruun Neergaard (1776–1824), published in 1820.

ABOVE On this general plan of Villa Pliniana from the nineteenth century, the architect Louis-Hippolyte Le Bas drew the elevation and the famous intermittent fountain described by Leonardo da Vinci. École nationale supérieure des beaux-arts, Paris.
FACING PAGE Ambrogio and Gregorio Zavattari, *The Marriage of Theodelinda and Agilulf* (detail), fresco, 1444. Duomo di Monza, Chapel of Theodelinda.

By the end of 194 BCE, the entire region had been pacified under the banner of Rome and took the name of Cisalpine Gaul. Comum was strengthened and rebuilt after a foray by the Reti and repopulated with three thousand colonists in 77 BCE. After draining the swampy areas, in 59 BCE the city was re-established with the name of Novum Comum in its current location on the shore of the lake by order of Julius Caesar, who probably saw it as a foothold for expansion of the empire across the Alps, given the strategic importance of the city and homonymous lake. Five thousand colonists, including five hundred noble Greeks, came to populate the new colony. It was at this time that the Via Regia road from Como to Summus Lacus was laid out along the western shore of the lake.

With the Romans came the use of Latin and Roman law and customs, and a great deal of urban development. Farming and trade flourished, and towns and cities sprang up and developed. Important cultural figures were born in this area: Pliny the Younger in Comum (Como) and the great poet Virgil (70–19 BCE) in Mantua. The population of Como grew significantly, and elegant buildings were erected, such as the baths and the library on the shores of the lake. Pliny the Younger would build his two villas, Comoedia and Tragedia, whose ownership is still contended by the lakeside municipalities. In the final centuries of the empire, Mediolanum (Milan), initially second to Brixia (Brescia), witnessed a significant increase in its political and religious importance because of its vicinity to the Alpine stretches of the Ticino River valley. With the episcopate of Ambrose (c. 340–397 CE), its importance grew further to the point where it became one of the seats of the tetrarchy during the reign of Constantine (272–337 CE). In 313, Constantine issued the famous Edict of Milan, releasing Christians from persecution and righting the wrongs done against them. Meanwhile, on Lake Como (or Lake Larius, as the Romans called it, possibly from the pre-Indo-European root "lar-", meaning "small valley" or "hollow"), the culture of beauty and villas continued to develop. We find evidence of this in a document fragment dating to 533–37 written by Cassiodorus (c. 485–580 CE), initially a Roman senator and later minister to King Theoderic (c. 454–526 CE): "The lake is contained in a very large and very deep valley ... around it are clustered, forming a sort of crown, splendid high mountain passes ... the shores embellished by villas ... surrounded by a perpetually green sash of olive groves."

In the final years of the Western Roman Empire, Lombardy's relative closeness to the confines along the Danube left it vulnerable to the numerous raids by Barbarians. When the empire collapsed, Ostrogoths and Byzantines alternated control of the territory. In 569, the Byzantines were defeated by a Germanic people hailing, according to the eighth-century historian Paulus Diaconus (c. 720–799 CE), from what is now Scandinavia: these were the Longobards, from which derives the name Lombardy. The early period of Longobard dominion was terrible for the Romans, who were persecuted mercilessly. On Lake Larius the

civilization of the villas was transformed: the cultured leisure time of intellectual pleasures gave way to the working of the land, which had become a resource to be exploited. However, the undeniable beauty of the landscape continued to be perceived and valued, as we read in these verses written by Paulus Diaconus in the eighth century in honor of the lake:

"It is always springtime with you because your green soil is always in blossom ... you are girded by olive groves on both shores ... the red of pomegranates shines amidst the lovely gardens ... the scent of myrtle berries fills the air ... the citron wreathes all with its perfume."

The villas of the late empire were replaced by simple farm buildings built of simple materials. It was in this period that a system of mixed farmlands and gardens became definitively established, favoring increasing interest in the botanical characteristics of the lakeshore, which would become one of the prevailing elements in the legend of the lake. Evergreen trees, citrus and olive groves, exotic and scented plant species, vineyards and fruit orchards: as part of a design, they are the projection of architecture onto the landscape. They bond human structures to the surrounding environment in the most harmonious way possible. And they laid the groundwork for an idealized relationship with the land, which would reach its apex more than a thousand years later in the eighteenth and nineteenth centuries.

But let us remain for a moment in the sixth century. The period of oppression by the Longobards ended when Queen Theodelinda (c. 570–627 CE) converted her people to Christianity: this ushered in a period of peace and cooperation that unfortunately

ABOVE Tintoretto (1518–1594), *Federico I Gonzaga Relieving the City of Legnano*, sixteenth century. Bayerische Staatsgemäldesammlungen, Munich.
FACING PAGE *Meeting between the Emperor Massimiliano I and Massimiliano Sforza.* Manuscript 2163, folio 6, of *Liber Iesus*, fifteenth century. Biblioteca Trivulziana, Milan.

would not last long. The Longobards entered into conflict with the Pope, who summoned another Barbarian people, the Franks, to his aid. This was the time of Charlemagne (c. 742–814 CE), who divided the land into fiefdoms and entrusted their administration to loyal nobles known as vassals, who governed the territory on his behalf, giving form to the feudal system of the early Middle Ages. In this period, Como maintained its supremacy in trade. In terms of its strategic importance, it became a frontier post initially to subdue the nearby Alpine peoples and then for the conquest of Germany. The Strada Regina ("Royal Road"), the old Via Regia that the Romans had built by joining preexisting paths, provided a land route to the Spluga and Maloja passes. But even more important was the water route offered by the lake. The Larian *nautae* (boatmen) belonging to the *Collegium Nautarum Comensium* (Lake Como shipping association) were the true masters of the lake, with the lake fleet under the control of the *Praefectus classis cum curis civitatis*, the civil and military authority in Como.

A new political model began to spread throughout northern Italy, and thus also in Lombardy, in the eleventh and twelfth centuries: the Medieval Commune. The model had many parallels with the ancient city states that had been the birthplace of direct democracy in Greece many centuries before. The communes were a sign of rebirth after the end of the first millennium and

C. Baruello
St. Abondio
S. Marta
S. Pietro Celestino
Bourg St. Rocca
Borgo du Port du Tour
St. Francois
la Ville de
COMO
A'AMSTERDAM
Chez P. MORTIER

St Jean
Colegio Golia
St Theresa
Pasque
P. Sala
LAC DE COMO

"About eight miles above Como is the Pliniana, which increases and ebbs every six hours, and its swell supplies water for two mills; and its ebbing makes the spring dry up."

Leonardo da Vinci, notebook entry, c. 1494–1502.

were the principle vehicle for a repopulation of the cities, which had slowly been emptying out after fall of the Western Roman Empire and the establishment of a feudal system. In Lombardy, the commune model and the desire to maintain independence from the imperial authorities led to the formation of the Lombard League, a military alliance among the various Lombard cities (and others as well) that defeated the troops of the emperor Frederick Barbarossa (1122–1190) during the Battle of Legnano in 1176. The Peace of Constance of 1183 substantially recognized the autonomy of a large group of Italian cities while subjecting the communes to fealty to the Holy Roman Emperor. In the twelfth century, the commune model began to come apart: the age of the *Signorie*—of grand aristocratic families—was beginning. From the twelfth to the fourteenth century, many Lombard cities fell under the control of aristocratic families: the Gonzaga in Mantua, and the Visconti and Sforza families in Milan. The families often summoned the most famous artists to embellish their palaces and cities, leading to the creation of such marvelous works of art as the Sforza Castle in Milan and the Ducal Palace in Mantua. Control of Lombardy was again contested in the late fifteenth century. The French initially seized control of the territory but the duchy of Milan later fell to the Spanish, who remained in Italy for a long time. During the period of Spanish dominion, after an initial period of prosperity, the region witnessed progressive decay, aggravated in the seventeenth century by the plague. The eastern part of the region fell under the control of the Venetian government in the fifteenth century: Bergamo, Crema, Brescia, and Salò thus had a history that was much different from the rest of the region up to 1797. Between the twelfth and the fourteenth century, also in the Larian region, relations between the cities and the countryside were dominated by the gradual concentration of rural ownership into the hands of the urban middle class. This favored the construction of seasonal dwellings on the shores of the lake for citizens and nobles, who stayed there during the summer or at certain times in the growing season, such as the grape harvest. Alongside and emulating these dwellings, the houses of local notables also became increasingly elegant. These were the conditions that opened up a new season of villas: structures dedicated to leisure time and the enjoyment of convivial company, which was not in short supply thanks to extensive residential neighborhoods and the rooms for guests. It was the beginning of a new chapter. ◆

PARTE ALPESRE DELLO STATO DI MILANO Con il Lago Maggiore di Lugano é di Como.
PARTE DE GRISONI.
LEPONTII.
Lago maggiore olim Verbanus Lacus
Lago di Lugano olim Gauni Lacus
Lago di Como olim Larius Lacus
Lago di Orta
Lago di Ghiuira
Val di Canobbiano
Bellinzona
Locarno
Lugano
Como
Varese
Arona
Angiera
Canobbio
Luino
Intra

PARTE ALPESTRE DELLO
STATO DI MILANO
Con il Lago Maggiore di
Lugano é di Como.
GRISONI.
LEPONTII.
Lago di Como olim Larius Lacus
Lacus Ceresius olim Lago di Lugano
Lago Maggiore olim Verbanus Lacus
Lago di Orta

PAGES 34–35 *Map of Como.* Engraving, 1570. Museo Civico Storico Giuseppe Garibaldi, Como.
OVERLAY Henricus Hondius (1597–1651), *Alpine region of the state of Milan with lakese Maggiore, Lugano, and Como*, seventeenth century.
ABOVE Lake access at Villa Melzi (Bellagio). Built in 1808-10, Villa Melzi is one of the most emblematic villas on the lake, having hosted such illustrious people as Eugène de Beauharnais, Stendhal, and Franz Liszt.
PAGES 38–39 The stone arch leading to the rose garden of Villa Balbiano.

VILLA BALBIANO THROUGH THE CENTURIES

Lake Como, at 56 square miles (145 km^2), is Italy's third largest (but unquestionably deepest) lake, but has only one small island: Comacina. It is located along the western shore in the western branch, a little south of the Bellagio promontory. Comacina is one-third of a mile long and 200 yards wide (600 x 200 m)—a small patch of land covered with trees, but filled with history. It is an important archaeological site with the ruins of a tower-residence, five Romanesque religious buildings, and an early Christian baptistery with Carolingian frescoes. It isn't surprising that this little scrap of land should be home to such old buildings: it is located along a route that has a long history of great importance. For centuries, Lake Como (or Lake Larius) represented the main communication route between Como and Chiavenna. Boats sailed north as far as Lake Mezzola, located between the tip of Lake Como and Chiavenna, and from here passengers and goods continued on to Switzerland and from there to the rest of Europe.

ABOVE Time seems to have stopped in the narrow streets of the charming villages around Villa Balbiano.
FACING PAGE Romanesque bell tower of the church of Santa Maria Maddalena in Ossuccio with Comacina Island in the background.

Parallel to the waterway there is also an ancient land road that was long a principal artery in a very old and dense network of historical, geographical, and cultural ties with the lands across the Alps. It was originally a network of trails, of secondary importance compared to the lake route, which was more practical and thus more traveled. This land route was developed in the Roman era, particularly during the imperial period, when its strategic importance grew. It would later be called the Strada Regina, a name documented for the first time in 1187. Between Comacina Island and the Strada Regina there is a small town called Ossuccio. It is one of the oldest settlements on the lake, as evidenced by a Roman votive altar dating to the second or third century CE, now found in the Romanesque church of Sant'Agata. As well as preserving evidence of the pagan cult, the altar also bears the name of the local inhabitants: Ausuciates. Moving eastward is the mouth of the Perlana River, where the surrounding area is named Balbiano. The first document referring to it by name—"*Murofracto sito Balbiani*"—dates to the year 941.

The great historian Paolo Giovio (1483–1552) wrote about Balbiano, formerly a ward of the Comacina island, as the place where his family owned houses and lands planted with mulberries and olives. Born in Como, Paolo Giovio was a physician, writer, humanist, and museologist *ante litteram*, but, most importantly, a politician and diplomat. There is little documentation of his youth. A devotee of linguistics, literary studies, and historiographical research, he distinguished himself as an elegant writer in Latin and, almost exclusively in his letters, also in the "vulgate", i.e. Italian. In 1536, Giovio initiated plans to build a villa in Borgovico, not far from Como, inspired by those of the great naturalist Pliny. He would use it as a museum to keep his immense collection of portraits of illustrious men: men of letters, artists, leaders, sovereigns. It wasn't a museum in the modern sense of the term, but rather a dwelling where he could surround himself with works of particular significance to him. He had the original idea of accompanying all the portraits with a biography of the person depicted. These biographies were then collected in his *Elogia*, which is considered, together with his *Historiae*, among the most important literary works of this great intellectual and politician.

The Giovio family had been one of the most influential in the parishes of Isola and Lenno since the previous century. In the thirteenth century, as reported in a document dated 1280, the family held the right of patronage (*jus patronatus*) to the Santa Maria Maddalena Hospital in Stabio, currently the part of the municipality of Ossuccio known as Ospedaletto, in the parish of Isola. In the second half of the fifteenth century, Luigi Giovio, Paolo's father, shared the right of patronage with his brothers.

ABOVE Antonio Maria Crespi (1580–1630), *Portrait of Paolo Giovio*, Italian historian and bishop. Biblioteca e Pinacoteca Ambrosiana, Milan.
FACING PAGE *Il Museo*, villa-museum built by Paolo Giovio in the sixteenth century in Borgo Vico, Como. He used it to exhibit his art collection and particularly the portraits of the famous men of his day. Musei Civici di Como, Como.

The family's estate at Balbiano had many trees, including olives, and vegetable gardens. The Perlana River, bordering the property, is normally placid but periodically floods and causes significant damage to the land around it: the "crumbling houses" that the historian writes about might have been in such condition precisely for this reason. In 1541, when Paolo Giovio went to Milan to honor the Holy Roman Emperor Charles V (1500–1558), he named as his procurator his nephew Cesare, the son of his older brother, Benedetto (1471–1545), who was also a historian. As attested in a deed drawn up by the notary Cristoforo Vaccani of Lenno at the Hospital of Stabio, on October 14 of the same year, acting in the name of his uncle, Cesare gave ownership of Balbiano to Francesco Giovio, the son of the late Battista, Paolo's uncle, and thus Cesare's first cousin once removed. The land is described as lying between the lake and the Strada Regina, and having a vineyard, an olive grove, and mulberry and fruit trees. It had an unfinished, roofless outbuilding and a house built by the historian's forebears: a two-story structure, with roof shingled in *piode* (the local flagstones), standing on a courtyard with a drinking well. A stone staircase led up to the first floor. The side toward the Perlana was semi-destroyed. This is where the villa would be built.

In 1596, Ottavio Giovio (Paolo's great-nephew, Benedetto's grandson), who had inherited the property, sold it to Tolomeo Gallio (1527–1607), nephew of a cardinal of the same name who had worked with Paolo Giovio, transcribing his *Elogia*. When his uncle died, Tolomeo inherited the Castle of Scaldasole and the title of count, later also acquiring the title of first Duke of Alvito, in the kingdom of Naples. The idea began to take shape in his mind of building a villa worthy of the family's new status at Balbiano. This was the beginning of a great metamorphosis. The name of the architect in charge of design has been lost: the

owner of the villa at the end of the eighteenth century, Giovan Battista Giovio (1748–1814), a descendant of Paolo, and also a scholar and historian, identified the architect as Pellegrino Tibaldi (1527–1596). But no other documents have been found to support this.

When Tolomeo died, the property was inherited by his son Francesco, who sold it in 1637 to another Gallio, Marco, abbot and another grandson of Cardinal Tolomeo. Marco Gallio was an art lover who had already built two villas just outside of Como, the Gallietta and the Gallia. At Balbiano, the abbot proceeded to rebuild the villa, which rose from the "magnificent ruins" described one century earlier by Paolo Giovio: he increased the height of the house and removed some of the partition walls on the ground floor, creating the large central salon, which is repeated, with a double-height ceiling, on the floor above. He embellished it with many carved stone ornaments, taking features of Villa Gallietta as his model. At his death, on August 13, 1638, the four outer walls of the villa with their gneiss plinth and most of the partition walls on the three floors had been built, but the finishing work had not been done. Only the cornice had been built for the roof.

Ownership of Balbiano then passed into the hands of Carlo Gallio, who, according to the testament drawn up on July 11, 1632,

ABOVE Giovanni Domenico Campiglia (1692–1768), portrait of the architect Pellegrino Tibaldi.
FACING PAGE AND PAGE 46 The landing on the third floor of the villa features the portraits of important Italian cardinals and popes from the sixteenth to the eighteenth century, including Tolomeo Gallio.

inherited most of the abbot's estate. As engraved on an eighteenth-century stone plaque placed in the villa, it was Carlo, marchese of Isola, who continued building the villa. The Lombard *cotto* flooring was finished, paintings and wallpaper were installed, and an outbuilding was rebuilt between the villa and the river. Carlo died on August 30, 1641, leaving the estate to his son Giacomo as his sole heir. Work continued. The villa now had two stairways: a "secret" one next to the north entrance, which would be rebuilt three centuries later, and the main staircase, which still stands. As we read on an eighteenth-century stone plaque on an interior wall, in 1680 the Marquis Giacomo Gallio celebrated the completion of the building, which he had enriched with prized stuccowork and frescoes, gardens and fountains. Household inventories record that the walls of the villa were decorated with a great many paintings. Gallio had cypresses planted in the garden on the upland side. The historian Anton Gioseffo Della Torre di Rezzonico (1709–1785) writes about the cypresses in the late eighteenth century, saying that they gave the estate, washed by the waters of Lake Como, a feeling of eternity. A drawing from 1778 shows that the century-old trees were planted in two parallel rows, creating a visually stunning lane connecting the front gate on the road to the second level of the garden in front of the villa.

In 1778, Giacomo Gallio's heirs, the dukes of Alvito, transferred Balbiano to Giovan Battista Giovio, in whose hands it would remain a mere nine years. Indeed, in 1787, the property, accompanied by a detailed plan of the villa and gardens, passed into the hands of Cardinal Angelo Maria Durini (1725–1796),

papal nuncio, a connoisseur of art and literature, art patron, and collector. The Durini family were wealthy merchants and bankers, one of the most important and influential families in Lombardy from the mid-seventeenth century through the eighteenth century. In 1648, they had acquired the countship of Monza and, that same year, the family palace in Milan, near San Babila, was completed based on designs by the architect Francesco Maria Richini (1584–1658).

Angelo Maria Durini was born in Milan in 1725, where he began his studies. He then moved to Rome, where he completed his education and embarked on his ecclesiastic career, later accompanying his uncle, the bishop Carlo Francesco Durini (1693–1767), to Paris. After returning to Rome, he earned a doctorate in civil and canon law, and in 1757 was named honorary prelate by Pope Benedict XIV (1675–1758) and member of the *Referendario delle due Segnature*, i.e. the court of grace and justice. After serving as Inquisitor in Malta and apostolic nuncio in Poland, he was appointed cardinal at the papal consistory of May 20, 1776, and placed at the head of the rich abbey of San Dionigi, with holdings in Milan and Merate, where Durini had a villa built for himself. On a rise opposite the Mirabello estate, the Durini family's villa in Monza, he had another villa built, the Mirabellino. Under Angelo Maria's stewardship, the Balbiano property grew and was secured (with the consolidation of the embankment along the Perlana). Neighboring properties were purchased, new frescoes were painted, engraved plaques were installed, a small church and a tower were built, and a lighthouse was raised to guide boats (it would collapse in the nineteenth century). After setting his house in order, Durini had a double pavilion built in a panoramic position at the top of a promontory to the east. It featured a central portico with three arches with a library on one side and a music room on the other. In honor of Balbiano, the cardinal dubbed the new estate Balbianino. Today it is known as Balbianello and is a Fondo Ambiente Italiano (FAI—Italian National Trust) site.

Angelo Maria Durini was a man with impressive ties in the late eighteenth century: when he was appointed cardinal he received congratulations from Maria Theresa of Austria (1717–1780), King Carlo III of Spain (1716–1788), Duke Vittorio Amedeo III of Savoy (1726–1796), and from the Archdukes Leopold II (1747–1792) and Ferdinand of Austria (1754–1806). An art patron and poetry lover, he befriended a great many men of letters, including two of the most brilliant minds in Milan at the time: Giuseppe Parini (1729–1799), who was a frequent guest at Villa Balbiano, and Pietro Verri (1728–1797). Durini spent more and more time at his lakeside retreat, and it would be here that he breathed his last, on April 28, 1796. The work he did on the villa and its gardens continued to arouse the admiration of travelers, who came in increasing numbers to visit this corner of the lake. But an era had come to a close.

When Cardinal Durini died, the villa and grounds passed to a nephew, Giacomo Durini, who modernized and improved it.

On April 5, 1815, he purchased new plots of land adjacent to Balbiano, but sold everything again—including the outbuildings and furnishings—just one week later to Giuseppe Sepolina of Milan. Ownership then passed on to Sepolina's daughter Giuseppina, who married an Austrian and moved to Vienna in the 1820s. In 1849, the entire property was sold to the lawyer Francesco Delmati, whose son Giuseppe sold it in 1872 to Gustav Salomon Gessner (1818–1884)—a textile industrialist based in Milan but originally from Zurich—who expanded the buildings and installed a spinning mill.

It was also around this time that one of the great novels of Italian literature was published: Alessandro Manzoni's (1785–1873) three-volume *I promessi sposi* (The Betrothed), first published in 1827, with a revised version in 1840–42, set in Milan and on Lake Como in the seventeenth century. Manzoni's descriptions of the landscape around the lake were made known

"That branch of the Lake of Como, which extends southwards between two unbroken chains of mountains, and is all gulfs and bays as the mountains advance and recede, narrows down at one point, between a promontory on one side and wide shore on the other, into the form of a river; and the bridge which links the two banks seems to emphasize this transformation even more, and to mark the point at which the lake ends and the Adda begins, only to become a lake once more where the banks draw farther apart again, letting the water broaden out and expand into new creeks and bays."

Alessandro Manzoni, *The Betrothed*, 1827.

to thousands of readers. It was not, however, the finest period in the long history of Villa Balbiano. In 1877, the historian Antonio Balbiani (1838–1889) wrote with some bitterness: "Where the magnificent and noble cardinal [Angelo Maria Durini] invited pleasure-seeking hangers-on and literati, now stands a spinning mill. And my! How many small palaces have shed their aristocratic pride, their character of feudal monuments, to become a modest manufacturer of spools as at Balbiano!" The lake, on the other hand, was booming. Its shores had become a must-see for travels in Italy. The grand villas that look out over it drew in

FACING PAGE Giuseppe Molteni (1800–1867), *Portrait of Alessandro Manzoni and View of Lecco*, 1835. Pinacoteca di Brera, Milan. Manzoni was one of Italy's preeminent authors, representative of a movement, *Verismo* (Italian for "realism"), which manifested itself in literature, opera, and painting.

writers, painters, and composers, among them Stendhal (1783–1842), Franz Liszt (1811–1886), and Gustave Flaubert (1821–1880). Intellectual salons were established, political meetings were held, and sentimental stories were woven and helped nourish the lake's fame. The heart of this artistic and social ferment were the villas: new ones were built and old ones remodeled to suit the new tastes of the times. Stendhal, longtime Lake Como habitué, wrote: "The palaces multiply amidst the greenery, on the slopes, and are reflected in the waters. It is an elegant, picturesque, and voluptuous manner of building."

Villa Balbiano's excessively stately past may have prevented it from taking part in the ebullience of the nineteenth century. The property was thus passed down from generation to generation, carried into the twentieth century as the Società Anonima Setificio di Balbiano (Balbiano Silk Works). The property was then split in two. The land to the west was sold and the factory with the spinning mill was destroyed in the 1930s. In 1940 the parapet and gate on the shore crumbled and sank into the lake. In 1960 the villa changed hands once again. The new proprietor was the German engineer Hermann Hartlaub, owner of a large construction company. He was to undertake the initial restoration work, entrusted to the Swiss engineer Enrico Vuilliomenet: mural paintings were brought back to light, floors were redone, and a false ceiling was removed to reveal decorated wooden floor

ABOVE Michele Fanoli (1807–1876), *The Departure of the Betrothed*, 1831. Musei Civici Eremitani, Padua. The image is from Manzoni's *The Betrothed*, one of the great classics of Italian literature.
FACING PAGE Francis Towne (c. 1740–1816), *Lake Como*, 1781. Lake Como was a favorite among eminent European romantic and landscape painters.
PAGES 52-53 Girolamo Mantelli di Cannobio, *View of Balbiano from Lake Como*, late 1700s. British Library, London.

beams. The secondary stairway was rebuilt and the garden was given new life with an Italian-style garden with rows of holly oaks, hedges, and statues between the entrance gate to the north and the villa.

In the meantime, however, something else was in the air. The postwar years brought not only reconstruction and the urgency of getting a defeated country back on its feet, but also something unexpected: the Italian Style, this unbeatable mix of tourism, style, cinema, and culture ushered in a new Grand Tour, but with a Pop influence: Italy was emerging as a fashion destination. The first fashion show took place in Florence in 1951, organized by Giovanni Battista Giorgini (1898–1971). Two years later the world would dream of a *Roman Holiday* together with Audrey Hepburn (1929–1993) and Gregory Peck (1916–2003). In 1960, Federico Fellini's (1920–1993) *La Dolce Vita* was such a worldwide hit that its title has become a common expression embodying the essence of Italian life. While the Autostrada del Sole (Highway of the Sun), inaugurated in 1964, began carrying Italians to the sea, the lakes and their villas remained as the last word in elegance. It is no surprise that Villa d'Este, in Cernobbio near Como, was chosen as the venue for the European House-Ambrosetti Forum, bringing together heads of state, Nobel laureates, businesspeople, and representatives of international institutions around the same table since 1975. The FAI (Italian National Trust) was also founded in 1975, taking its cues from the National Trust in Britain to safeguard Italy's architectural, artistic, and landscape heritage. Its properties include Villa del Balbianello, the eighteenth-century companion to Villa Balbiano, built by Cardinal Durini. The shores of Larius also witnessed the arrival of a young fashion designer from Calabria at about that same time: he often came to visit the

silk mills around Como and fell in love with the atmosphere. His name was Gianni Versace (1946–1997), and in 1980 he bought Villa Le Fontanelle, near Moltrasio, filling his new abode with early and contemporary art to the point where it was almost a museum. And with him came famous friends, parties, journalists. After the splendors of the nineteenth century, a new, marvelous season was beginning on the lake. In 1982, Villa Balbiano was bought by Michele Canepa, an industrialist in the silk business. He embellished the villa with a collection of art prints of Lake Como, as well as numerous works of contemporary art and period furniture, and he beautified the gardens with new species of trees and flowers, some quite rare. He would take the villa into the new century, and into a new chapter in its history. ◆

ABOVE Johann Jakob Falkeisen (1804–1883), *The Tremezzina Shore from the Loggia of Villa del Balbianello*, nineteenth century. Biblioteca Nazionale Marciana, Venice.
FACING PAGE Panoramic loggia above Villa del Balbianello built in 1787 by Cardinal Angelo Maria Durini. This elegant structure was intended for rest and the pleasures of writing and conversation.
PAGES 56-57 C. Bosetti, *Group of Men in a Boat*, 1890, with Villa Melzi in Bellagio in the background.

GALATEA

THE HUMANIST DREAM OF CARDINAL DURINI

Deep in the heart of Milan's elegant Brera district is one of Italy's oldest art schools: the Accademia di Belle Arti di Brera (Brera Academy of Fine Arts), founded by Maria Theresa of Austria in 1776. The palazzo housing it is a former convent reworked several times over the course of its history and renovated in the late eighteenth century by the renowned architect Giuseppe Piermarini (1734–1808). Here students and scholars cultivate their minds through the study of the arts (painting, sculpture, and set design) and the sciences. The Academy also features an astronomical observatory and a botanical garden, as well as one of Italy's most eminent libraries, the Braidense, open to the public since 1786.

In July 1795, the grand staircase leading to the library was bustling with men carrying heavy crates filled with books. The books were part of a generous private donation of some three thousand volumes, almost all of them prized editions, including a number of rare and important manuscripts. This was the gift of Cardinal Angelo Maria Durini to his city. Many of the books had come from his beloved Villa Balbiano, where Durini passed away in April 1796, while the others had been at Mirabello, the family villa in Monza. More than a donation, this collection was a cultural testament: "To you, Brera, I have given my books ... to you, without remorse, because I die and pass away, but you instead are rich and grand and glorious and remain eternally," he wrote in his dedication.

The noble Milanese prelate was one of the cultural and political protagonists of his time, a paragon of Lombard aristocracy in the Age of Enlightenment, upholding the most conservative values but open to European intellectual exchange.

Learning had always exercised an enormous fascination for the cardinal. As a boy he had been an excellent and impassioned student at the Barnabite school in Milan. He was particularly fond of rhetoric, grammar, elocution, classical literature, and, most of all, Latin elegiac poetry—in his adult years he often composed

FACING PAGE Giosuè Sala (1784–1814), *Portrait of Cardinal Angelo Maria Durini*, c. 1778. Civiche Raccolte d'Arte, Pinacoteca, Monza.
PAGE 60 The historian Pietro Verri (left) and the poet Giuseppe Parini (right), friends of Cardinal Durini, were two of the many men of letters who frequented Villa Balbiano.

occasional poetry in the language of ancient Rome, which the Lombard aristocracy favored as the idiom for literary pursuits.

Cardinal Durini was a very erudite man, a bibliophile, and, most importantly, a dedicated patron of the arts and literature, as witnessed by his friendships with the great Lombard men of letters of the eighteenth century, including the poet Giuseppe Parini (1729–1799), who dedicated his lengthy ode *La Gratitudine* to the Cardinal in 1791, the writer and historian Pietro Verri (1728–1797), the politician and art collector Karl von Firmian (1718–1782), and the dialectal poet Domenico Balestrieri (1714–1780). These friendships explain the many first editions by these authors—all brilliant minds in the cultural milieu of the time—in Durini's Braidense bequest.

Durini was also very interested in scientific and social progress: he wrote laudatory verses about subjects as varied as Copernicus, the balloon flight of the Montgolfier brothers, and Maria Theresa's reform of the University of Pavia. He was thus strongly rooted in classical culture, but still deeply involved in his own time, as is demonstrated by his intense diplomatic activity covering almost twenty years, from 1756 to 1776, in missions to Rome, Malta, Poland, and Avignon.

In 1776, Pope Pius VI elevated him to Cardinal Priest. But Durini, who was fifty-one years old at the time, had already decided to withdraw into private life in his magnificent Lombard residences, the villas Mirabello and Mirabellino near Monza, and Balbiano and Balbianello on Lake Como. Mirabellino and Balbianello, in particular, were built by the cardinal as a retreat

FACING PAGE Peter Birmann (1758–1844), *View of Villa Balbiano*, 1806, and *View of Villa del Balbianello*, 1807. Camera di Commercio, Industria, Artigianato e Agricoltura, Como. These two drawings document the original state of the two residences before they were remodeled by Cardinal Durini.

*"To you, Brera, I have given my books ...
to you, without remorse, because I die and pass away,
but you instead are rich and grand and
glorious and remain eternally."*

Cardinal Angelo Maria Durini, 1795.

for poets, artists, and intellectuals, his illustrious guests and friends. These villas thus embodied the image of an ideal, perfect world, a place illuminated by the light of the intellect, taste, and beauty—in short, the dream of an extraordinary man.

In her monograph *Il cardinale Angelo Maria Durini (1725–1796), un mecenate lombardo nell'Europa dei Lumi fra arte, lettere e diplomazia* (Cardinal Angelo Maria Durini, a Lombard patron in the Europe of Enlightenment between art, letters, and diplomacy), Cristina Geddo writes: "Durini is a man of paradoxes, capable of merging old and new, conservatism and progressivism. In him dwell the opulent, bon-vivant cardinal, the sworn adversary of Voltaire, the cosmopolitan diplomat, the impenitent Arcadian, the humanist, and the unshakeable Latinist alongside the scholar of the Lombard dialect and homeland, the rebel nuncio champion of Polish liberty, the democrat and feminist *ante litteram*, and lastly the patron of the Lombard luminaries and the first to celebrate them in a modern pantheon of contemporary illustrious men." ◆

ABOVE Coat of arms of Angelo Maria Durini. Bibliothèque municipale, Avignon.
FACING PAGE Eighteenth-century Lombard painter (Paolo Borroni?), *Apotheosis of Cardinal Durini on Mount Parnassus*, c. 1778. Private collection.
PAGES 64–65 Created on the initiative of Cardinal Durini, this black Varenna marble plaque surmounted by the family emblem commemorates the cardinal's purchase of the property as a place of leisure for himself and his friends.

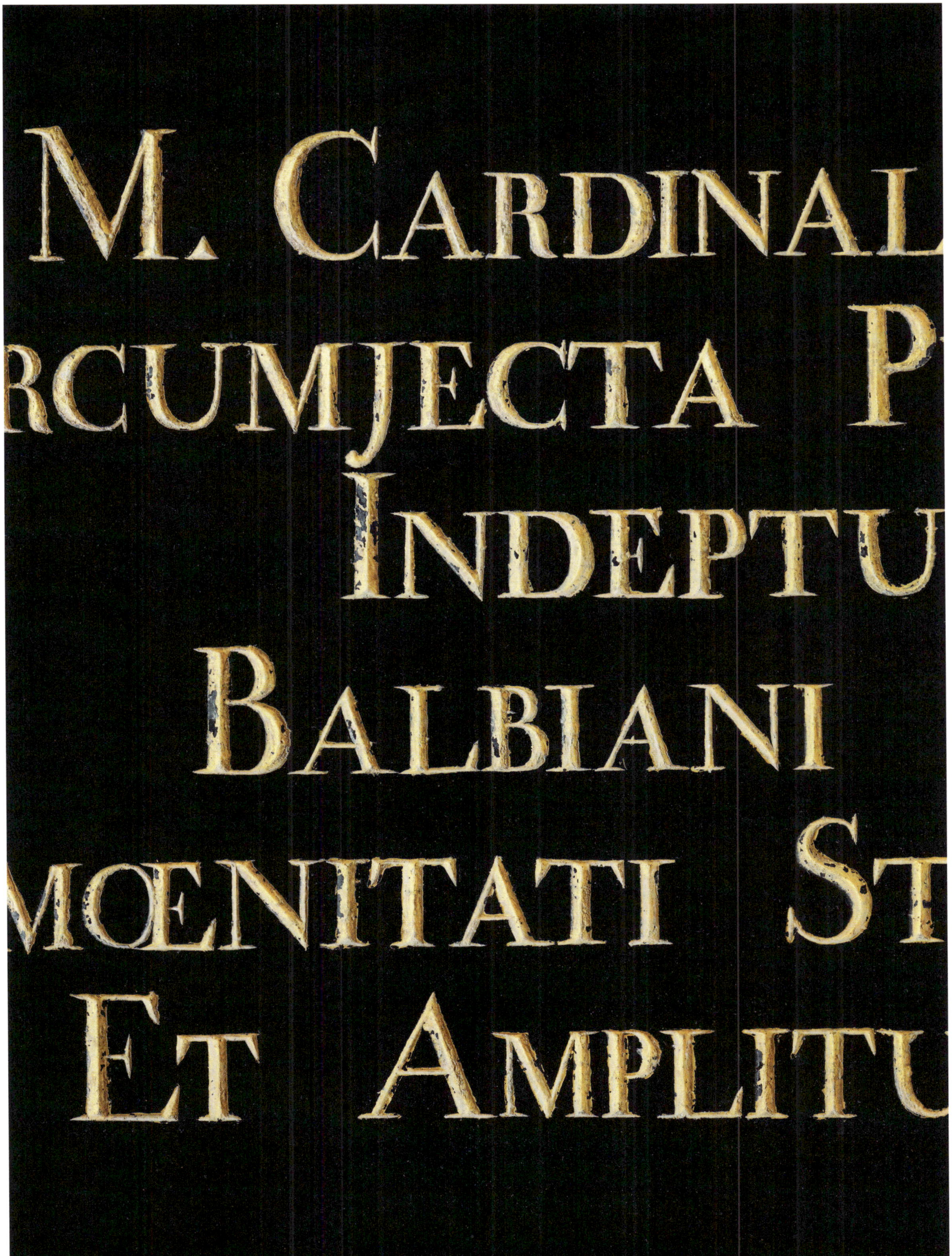
M. CARDINAL
RCUMJECTA P
INDEPTU
BALBIANI
MŒNITATI ST
ET AMPLITU

II

AN ENCHANTING DESTINATION

THE ETERNAL BEAUTY OF LARIO

For twenty centuries the shores of Lake Como—known locally as Lario—richly evocative and wreathed in their own special beauty, have enchanted travelers of all hue: royalty and heads of state, artists, writers, and composers such as Napoleon, Winston Churchill, Wolfgang Goethe, Lord Byron, Gustave Flaubert, Henry Wadsworth Longfellow, Hermann Hesse, and Richard Wagner, just to name a few.

Books have been written here, works of art have been painted, and enthralling music composed. Legend has it that Gioacchino Rossini wrote the opera *Tancredi* in just three days while staying at Villa Pliniana. The area has also provided the setting for great love affairs, such as that between Albert Einstein and Mileva Maric, who vacationed on the lake in the spring of 1901. The great physicist wrote to her of a special sort of magic: "You must come to visit me in Como.... You will see by yourself how lively and cheerful I've become and my frown finally is finished."

The lake continues to be an exclusive tourist destination, drawing people from all over the world for its mild climate and natural, timeless setting, so distant from the troubles of the world and the tyranny of the ticking clock. Stately historical dwellings, luxuriant gardens, age-old mountain paths, enchanting villages, and luxury hotels contribute to its restorative serenity, which is accentuated by festivals of jazz and classical music, literature, and visual arts hosted in Como or Bellagio.

Lario became particularly lively at the turn of the twentieth century, when it became *de rigueur* for worldly cultural and social circles to visit and a favorite meeting spot for world leaders. The villas, of course, were at the very heart of this artistic and social ferment. Buildings and palazzi were newly erected or remodeled to suit the tastes of the time.

The twentieth century also ushered in major revolutions of style that left significant traces up and down the lake: Giuseppe Terragni, a native of Como and one of the most important architects of Italian "constructive rationalism"—a nascent embrace of

FACING PAGE Spiral columns on the balustrade are one of the ornamental characteristics of Villa Monastero in Varenna.
PAGES 70–71 The famous cypresses at Villa Balbiano; the majestic stairway in the Italian garden at Villa Sommi, Lecco.

modernity in architecture driven by Marinetti's futurist doctrine—saw some of his most famous works built here. In the 1940s, Comacina Island became home to a colony of artists who lived in small wood and stone studio-cabins combining the local building tradition with the principles of Le Corbusier. Recently restored, they remain beautiful and valuable documents of a particular period in time.

Lake Como has been a favorite destination of the international jet set and stars of the silver screen since the 1920s. In mid-decade, Alfred Hitchcock chose Villa d'Este (Cernobbio) as the setting for his debut film *The Pleasure Garden*. And it is also said that Orson Welles was here when he wrote *The Lady from Shanghai*. Villa del Balbianello is probably the most sought-after movie location; its fantastic scenery probably has something to do with it. A long list of movies has been filmed here, including

Piccolo mondo antico (1941, with Alida Valli), *The Charterhouse of Parma* (1947), *A Month by the Lake* (1995, with Uma Thurman and Vanessa Redgrave), *Star Wars, Episode II: Attack of the Clones* (2002), and *Casino Royale* (2006).

The villas that dot the Larian shores are emblems of a glorious history and are eternally welcoming. The Region of Lombardy's Cultural Heritage Registry lists seventy-one of them, all of significant historic and artistic value, many associated with important people who have stayed or lived in them, heightening their timeless, universal allure. As the Italian architect and writer, Camillo Boito, wrote in 1884: "As for Lake Como, who doesn't know it? Who has not dreamed of having a small villa there with a garden and a little boat tied up at the dock?" ◆

FACING PAGE View of Lake Como from Villa Carlotta, Tremezzina, renowned for its botanical garden and the many masterpieces of art in its interiors.
ABOVE Villa Pizzo, built on a promontory between Cernobbio and Moltrasio, is only visible from the lake, against the backdrop of an extensive park filled with luxuriant Mediterranean vegetation and venerable old trees.

FACING PAGE Andrew Zega and Bernd H. Dams,
Rose Garden Arch, watercolor, 2018.
FOLDOUT Andrew Zega and Bernd H. Dams,
Façade of Villa Balbiano, watercolor, 2018.

"On the Lavedo promontory at Balbiano, which offers beautiful panoramas, Cardinal Durini built a beautiful house, a small, well-decorated church, a fine mooring, and a lighthouse to guide sailors. The place is located at the mouth of the Perlana river. Following the river upstream, one enters a very wild and picturesque valley."

Johann Jakob Wetzel, *Picturesque Journey to Lake Como*, 1819.

FACING PAGE Entrance to the rose garden through the late-seventeenth-century stone arch.

III

CULTIVATED ECLECTICISM IN THE DÉCOR

A NEW SEASON: THE INTERIORS

And thus, amidst crumbling buildings, shifts in use and fashion, and the unexpected twists of history, Balbiano enters the twenty-first century. In 2011, the new owners hired the internationally famous French interior architect Jacques Garcia to modernize the property. He teamed with Carlota Proença de Almeida, who was responsible for renovation and restoration. The goal of the complex, comprehensive project was to raise the comfort level of the villa without compromising any of its historical charm or authenticity. They succeeded in installing new electrical, heating, air conditioning, and plumbing systems in a completely unobtrusive way and brought the historic landmark back to its original magnificence.

The villa traces its origins back to the sixteenth century. Historical documentation was patchy at best, so the architects had quite a challenge envisioning how it had once looked. By sifting through the available information—title deeds or records of work done over the centuries—they were able to reconstruct the events and developments that had affected the appearance of the villa over the course of its life. While the villa had generally stayed true to its origins, standing solidly with sober elegance in its lakeside setting, the addition of an extra story had altered both its interior and exterior structure. Few months of historical research were necessary to obtain authorization to proceed from the Superintendency of Architectural and Landscape Heritage.

Originally, the plan was to focus on the interior decoration, by Jacques Garcia. However, the discovery of earlier embellishments (seventeenth- and eighteenth-century mural paintings) beneath those initially visible demanded a radical rethink. It was no longer a simple question of embellishing and improving the comfort of the villa, but of preserving and restoring these newly discovered vestiges of the past.

PAGES 82–83 Villa Balbiano, approached from the main gate.
FACING PAGE The façade on the lake side repeats the gray stone motif decorating the front door.
PAGES 86–87 The Sala delle Colonne features seventeenth-century frescoes by Giovan Paolo and Raffaele Recchi. The ceremonial straight-backed armchairs on either side of the console tables were crafted in Rome in the late eighteenth century, influenced by the rococo style.

The villa exhibits a classic geometry: it is a simple and straightforward rectangular volume allowing a number of circulation paths among the various rooms on each floor. The rooms had been partitioned, so the project entailed reestablishing their original configuration without altering the sequence of doorways. This resulted in the creation of very large bathrooms in spaces that had previously been used for other purposes.

The study of the architecture's evolution led to an interesting discovery: the rooms on the ground floor were richly designed while those on the upper floors were painted in uniform colors or wallpapered. It was only in what is now the master suite on the second floor that the original decorations were still visible. The bathrooms had been redone over the years, often with modern tiles, but it seemed highly unlikely that there had been no original embellishment. An investigation was thus undertaken, involving the painstaking removal and testing of layers of paint. This initially yielded few results, and so the work was resumed in a second phase, revealing three layers of mural painting applied in different periods. Renovation was undertaken based on these findings. In some cases, almost all layers of paint or wallpaper were removed and the underlying decorations restored, while in others, the original designs identified in the research were simply reproduced by the architects. Nothing was eliminated or lost.

The same careful refurbishment was applied to the floors. In the building work carried out in the 1960s, almost all the flooring materials had been removed and replaced with stone of relatively modest aesthetic value. Here, too, the decision was made to use a material closer to what had been used originally, either Bourgogne stone or Lombard *cotto*, depending on the room. These historical, recovered materials were laid over an underfloor heating system.

Although much was unquestionably lost or covered up, it would be a mistake to assume that all alterations made to the villa over the course of its life have been negative. For example, there used to be a vaulted ceiling over the salon on the second floor, probably an element of some architectural value. But with it, the salon had been an enclosed, even perhaps oppressive space. Its elimination in the nineteenth century allowed light to enter from above, greatly improving illumination.

The exterior also received a great deal of attention, starting with a major repair of the roof. The initial phase of work involved strengthening and reinforcing the frame members. However, the most demanding part of the project proved to be the restoration of the slabs of local stone. The roof had not been touched since the nineteenth century at the latest—perhaps even earlier. The slabs, made of a type of schist known locally as *piode*, were

FACING PAGE Detail of the eighteenth-century fresco depicting an escutcheon with the emblem of the Gallio family flanked by two cherubs.
ABOVE The roof of the villa, restored using authentic historical materials and techniques.
PAGES 90-91 The Sala delle Colonne is the heart of the villa, giving access on either side to the two wings.

crumbling. The architects were only able to gauge the state of deterioration when workers began to remove them: more than half of them were no longer usable. This introduced another problem since the original quarry was now depleted and stones with identical characteristics could no longer be found. However, an investigation of the quarry revealed a new vein containing a very similar stone that was a perfect match.

This type of roofing material is disappearing: *piode* tiles may measure as much as 6½ ft (2m) long by 3 ft (1m) wide, and thus require a robust supporting structure, which comes at considerable cost. Traditional slate, therefore, which can be industrially produced in small sizes, is increasingly chosen as a replacement. The reproduction of the original roof is a symbol of the unconventional and courageous approach needed to preserve the authentic original materials. This spirit also extended to improvements on the eaves. Where sections of copper rain gutter needed to be replaced, the new gutters were subjected to an aging process so they would perfectly match the preexisting elements. The exterior plaster and finishing also required special consideration. The exterior is not painted; instead, layers of lime plaster were applied by hand to create a natural, timeworn effect, with color varying depending on the time of day and the quality of the light. The handling of the plaster, roof, and treatment of the copper rain gutters at Villa Balbiano are now cited by the Superintendency as benchmarks of the highest-quality restoration work.

Villa Balbiano has been reborn. Its rooms have regained their stately magnificence and its decorations harmonize beautifully with its timeless setting—luxuriant vegetation and the limpid expanse of water encircled by mountains.

An ideal itinerary for discovering the villa begins on the ground floor—the original and oldest part of the villa—in the rooms and halls painted with mural paintings by renowned

"When you write the story of two happy lovers, let the story be set on the banks of Lake Como.... Here a man can breathe freely, surrounded by friendly nature, and his harmonious relationship with it is not disturbed by gigantic masses. He can love, or he can empty his mind and relax, since all he seems to be doing is enjoying his share of the general bliss."

Franz Liszt, letter to Louis de Ronchaud, September 20, 1837.

FACING PAGE The villa features many Chinese artifacts, such as the large eighteenth-century porcelain vase from the Qianlong period (r. 1736–95) in the center of the room.
PAGES 94-95 This mid-seventeenth-century Dutch cabinet features doors decorated with an elaborate Japanese landscape in gold lacquer and finely handcrafted hinges. Detail from a companion cabinet: a fish surfacing amidst the waves, carved in relief and again finished in gold lacquer.

"I'd return often to this sublime lake; no other sight in the whole world's as beautiful, at any rate to my heart. What's the point of going so far away to find happiness, it's here, within my reach!"

Stendhal, *The Charterhouse of Parma*, 1839.

eighteenth-century Italian artists such as Giovan Antonio Torricelli and his school. The Sala delle Colonne, heart of the villa, features splendid late seventeenth-century frescoes by Giovan Paolo and Raffaele Recchi, and four late eighteenth-century frescoed busts by Francesco and Gaetano Cartosio.

Entering the villa, the eye is immediately drawn to the Sala Durini, so-named because of the coat of arms of Cardinal Durini emblazoned on the ceiling. Originally the study, it has now become the library. Three beautiful bookcases are filled with historical volumes that transport us back in time; indeed, this was where the erudite cardinal liked to receive eminent artists and writers. The warm and intimate atmosphere of these encounters is still palpable today.

The library leads to the Sala dell'Arco di Tito, with splendid mural paintings by Torricelli on all four walls and the ceiling. This richly colored room provides access to one of the newly invented spaces created in the project: an indoor swimming pool looking out onto the garden through plate-glass windows installed in archways. The vaulted ceiling was inspired by the aviary at Villa Borghese in Rome. The two blank walls at either end are adorned with enchanting landscape scenes: an imaginary *veduta* of Lake Como on the opposite wall as you enter, while behind you is a panorama of Sorrento including Villa Astor, which also belongs to the owners of Villa Balbiano, based on a nineteenth-century painting of the villa.

The other ground-floor wing contains a very special and intimate space: Durini's chapel. Damaged and stripped bare over the centuries, it has now been brought back to its original form and meditative peace. The paintings on the walls and ceiling are the only surviving elements from the original chapel, while all the furnishings—paintings, icons, the tabernacle, a bas relief—were acquired specifically by the owners to recreate its special spiritual atmosphere.

The other spaces of note on the ground floor are the richly muraled dining room and the patio, particularly prized by the

FACING PAGE A pair of green porcelain vases from the Kangxi period (r. 1662–1722) sit on a heavy Rosso Levante marble table crafted in the late eighteenth century.
PAGES 98–99 The fireplace features two Louis XVI polished steel and gilded bronze andirons. It was in the period of Louis XIII that these practical log supports were elevated to the status of decorative elements.

owners for its romantic atmosphere, blending the warm colors of stone with the purple of the wisteria blossoms. It is a peaceful area, a natural extension of the villa to the outdoors.

The salon looking out onto the lake features a grand staircase leading up to the second floor. Here you enter a beautiful gallery featuring seventeenth-century stucco eagles made by Agostino Silva di Morbio. They were the object of painstaking work to reveal the full splendor of their plumage, surrounding leaves, and all other details that had become obscured over time. Layers and layers of paint filling in the hollows of the bas relief were also removed. The master bedroom, accessed from the gallery, still features its original décor even though it is difficult to determine its historical period. Characterized by a large scarlet damask bed and richly coffered ceiling, the bedroom is separated from the bathroom by an open-plan dressing room, where we find a door leading to a romantic terrace on the roof over the indoor pool, offering unparalleled view of the lake.

The central room on the second floor is the music room, featuring a double-height ceiling and a grand piano. There is also a large stone fireplace above which is a sculpted coat of arms. The third-level and the attic balcony railings are original. A door on the other side of the music room leads to a second suite dominated by an impressive wardrobe. Theatrically ornate with its Coromandel lacquerware panels, it acts as a screen between the dressing room and the bathroom.

The third-floor landing opens onto an exceptional suite, whose original wooden door symbolizes its unique character. Its views of the lake are the most breathtaking of any in the villa and its bathroom is the only one with white fixtures. The interior motif in the bathroom is based on its historical white Carrara marble bathtub and was used as the model for all the others. These immense bathrooms have been completely reinvented and faced in marble of different colors from various sources. The master bathroom is distinguished by its amazonite interior scheme with sinks, custom made by a French artisan, set upon massive vintage sculpted and gilded wooden consoles, and nineteenth-century mirrors.

The general furnishing scheme in the villa is marked by a cultivated eclecticism. While the owners sought to preserve all the existing furnishings, they were not afraid to add to them, thus creating a unique mix of genres, styles, and periods. They are also connoisseurs of Chinese art, and Eastern pieces sit comfortably amidst Empire or Louis XIV styles. The artful use of original elements from the villa (colors, frescoes, drawings) is equally remarkable: the intense shades of velvet, the choice of furniture, and the trimmings complement or contrast with the

FACING PAGE The purple velvet Marie Antoinette armchair dating to the Louis XVI period stands in the entry to the Sala del Tempietto.
PAGES 102–103 Architectural perspectives painted in the Sala della Colonna Traiana by Giovan Antonio and Grandonio Brenni in 1778.

*"Thy lofty steeps, and pathways roofed with vines,
Winding from house to house, from town to town,
Sole link that binds them to each other; walks
League after league, and cloistral avenues,
Where silence dwells if music be not there."*

William Wordsworth, "The Prelude," 1850.

mural paintings, showcasing an ornamental richness within the architectural simplicity of the villa. Many of the beds are historical. Made to the scale of earlier times, they all had to be lengthened by skilled artisans from the Como area.

The technical systems, which keep the house running and ensure total comfort, were installed under the roof during the initial phase of work and employ an excellent stratagem: they are all raised off the floor on dampers to prevent any noise or vibrations from being transmitted to the lower floors.

Returning down the secondary stairway, an addition from the 1960s, we enter the service zones. A cleverly hidden elevator serves these areas. The ground-floor area was created during the final phase of work. The professionally equipped kitchen zone and pantry adjoin the fitness room, and open onto the patio. This domestic space was carved out of humble, neglected rooms that had been used as storage spaces. Now, with its clean lines and warm and sophisticated materials such as wood, Lombard *cotto*, stainless steel, and Marquina marble, it has become a perfect complement to the historical parts of the villa.

Inspired by the eclectic nature of the Italian Renaissance—a taste for the old and a yen for the new—the owners and designers succeeded in striking a perfect balance between the history and heritage of Villa Balbiano and the most advanced technology, creating a comfortable dwelling of the rarest elegance that is a paean to the art of living. ◆

FACING PAGE The many fireplaces in Villa Balbiano contribute to creating a warm, relaxed atmosphere.
PAGES 106-107 This series of Chinese vases and other Chinese artifacts scattered throughout the villa testify to the influence of Far Eastern art in eighteenth-century Europe.

ABOVE AND FACING PAGE Details of architectural perspectives painted in the Sala della Colonna Traiana.
PAGES 110–111 The ceiling of the Sala del Tempietto presents a roof decorated with vines of red leaves, baroque curls, and acanthus.

FACING PAGE The Sala del Tempietto is an invitation to relax and meditate. The refined Louis XVI tea table, reminiscent of the work of Adam Weisweiler, is accompanied by two Marie Antoinette armchairs of the same epoch, upholstered in velvet and bearing the stamp of Louis-Madeleine Pluvinet, a late-eighteenth-century Parisian cabinet-maker.

"The Lake of Como*, the two moonlight villas,*
and the Farewell, *had prepared me for all that was beautiful*
and right in the terraced gardens, proportioned arcades,
and white spaces of sunny wall, which have in general no honest
charm for the English mind. But to me, they were almost
native through Turner—familiar at once, and revered. I had no idea
then of the Renaissance evil in them; they were associated
only with what I had been told of the 'divine art'
of Raphael and Lionardo."

John Ruskin, *Praeterita*, 1885.

PAGE 113, FACING PAGE, AND PAGE 116 The Sala del Tempietto with a mural painting by Giovan Antonio Torricelli representing an early temple, 1778.
PAGE 117 A rare Japanese Namban cabinet in lacquered wood from the Momoyama period (late sixteenth century) stands on a northern European carved wooden table (late seventeenth century).

"The palaces stand numerous amidst the greenery of the hills and are reflected in the waters. It's too much to call them palaces, but calling them country houses is not enough. It is an elegant, picturesque, sensuous type of construction, typical of the three lakes and the hills of Brianza."

Stendhal, from *Villa Melzi on Lake Como*, July 18, 1817.

PAGES 118-119 AND FACING PAGE The Sala dell'Arco di Tito gets its name from the eighteenth-century painting by Giovan Antonio Torricelli decorating the walls. An octagonal table in gilded wood with a pink and gray granite top occupies the center of the room. Originally in a Milanese palazzo, this nineteenth-century French table is a mix of rocaille and classical styles. To the right is a Napoleon III stool in gilded wood with structure mimicking a tasseled rope. Behind it is an early nineteenth-century copy of the *Venus de' Medici* in white Italian marble. This statue, from the fourth century BCE, shows the relationship of Venus and marine elements, represented by the dolphin at the side.

FACING PAGE AND ABOVE Strongly influenced by the fashion of the Grand Tour in the early decades of the eighteenth century, painters found architecture and ancient Roman ruins to be subjects with strong evocative and decorative potential.

ABOVE AND FACING PAGE Sala del Durini is the first room encountered by the visitor entering the villa. Its name derives from the cardinal's emblem painted on the ceiling. Originally an office, it is now an elegant library.
PAGES 126–127 The multi-volume sets of the *Dictionnaire des sciences* and the *Histoire universelle*, published in the nineteenth century, recall Cardinal Durini's intellectual nature. He was fond of entertaining writers and artists in his villa.

DICTIONNAIRE DES SCIENCES
TOM I
TOM II
TOM III
TOM IV
TOM V
TOM VI
TOM IX
HISTOIRE UNIVERSELLE
MÉMOIRES DU DUC DE SAINT-SIMON
TOM XXV
TOM XXVI
TOM XXVII
TOM XXVIII
TOM XXIX
TOM XXX

ABOVE, PAGES 130-132 The dining room is embellished with grand, atmospheric, eighteenth-century paintings by Giuseppe Porro, representing ancient architecture. It also features a number of baroque decorative elements, such as an original parapet in trompe-l'oeil porphyry.
FACING PAGE The silverware is laid on the carved and gilded mahogany and bronze table, from the late Louis XVI period.

ABOVE AND PAGES 134–135 Detail of an eighteenth-century French chandelier hanging over the dining table.
PAGE 136 Detail of the dining room.
PAGE 137 An architectural *capriccio* of classical ruins with Alexander visiting the tomb of Achilles by Giuseppe Zocchi (1711–1767).

DIVO CAROLO BORROMEO
ANG. CARDINALIS DVRINIVS
DICAVIT

FACING PAGE The chapel in the villa was created by Cardinal Durini in honor of Cardinal Carlo Borromeo (1538–1584). It was carefully restored by the owners to preserve its authenticity.
ABOVE Detail of the *Madonna and Child with Saint Joseph* from the workshop of Benvenuto di Giovanni, fifteenth century.

COLLOCUTIO
QUOQ
ÆVO INGRAV
ANNO

POSUIT SIBI ET AMICIS
COLLOCUTIONESQUE IN UMBRA
ÆVO INGRAVESCENTI PROSPICIENS

PAGES 140–141 The indoor pool was added during the restoration of the villa. It opens onto the garden and Lake Como through glassed-in arcades in the two side walls.
FACING PAGE A pair of Japanese Imari porcelain vases from the early eighteenth century each standing on a console table made of carved and gilded wood and marble. Italian works from the early eighteenth century, these consoles are typical of Roman baroque art.
ABOVE A seventeenth-century stucco eagle decorating the top of a column reflected in a vintage mirror. The stucco eagles in the villa were commissioned by Giacomo Gallio from the sculptor Agostino Silva di Morbio (1628–1706).
PAGES 144–145 View of Lake Como from the villa. Detail of the oil painting *Venus and Adonis* (1666) by the Flemish painter Theodoor van Thulden (1606–1669).

ABOVE An element of the Gallio family and the Durini coat of arms, the eagle is a recurring figure in the decorations of Villa Balbiano.
FACING PAGE Detail of a marble bust of Alexander the Great adorning one of the stairways in the villa, sculpted by Francesco Lazzarini (1748–1808).

"No sound of wheels or hoof-beat breaks
The silence of the summer day,
As by the loveliest of all lakes
I while the idle hours away.
I pace the leafy colonnade,
Where level branches of the plane
Above me weave a roof of shade
Impervious to the sun and rain.
At times a sudden rush of air
Flutters the lazy leaves o'erhead,
And gleams of sunshine toss and flare
Like torches down the path I tread.
By Somariva's garden gate
I make the marble stairs my seat,
And hear the water, as I wait,
Lapping the steps beneath my feet."

Henry Wadsworth Longfellow, "Cadenabbia," 1876–79.

FACING PAGE A large Dutch giltwood Stadtholder's chair, mid-eighteenth century. The green velvet with stumpwork embroidery in metal thread of the coat of arms of William Charles Henry, Prince of Orange-Nassau, afterwards William IV Stadtholder of the Netherlands (1711–1751).
PAGES 150–151 One of the black marble plaques firmly establishing Cardinal Durini's name in the history of Balbiano. View of the gardens from the second floor of the villa.

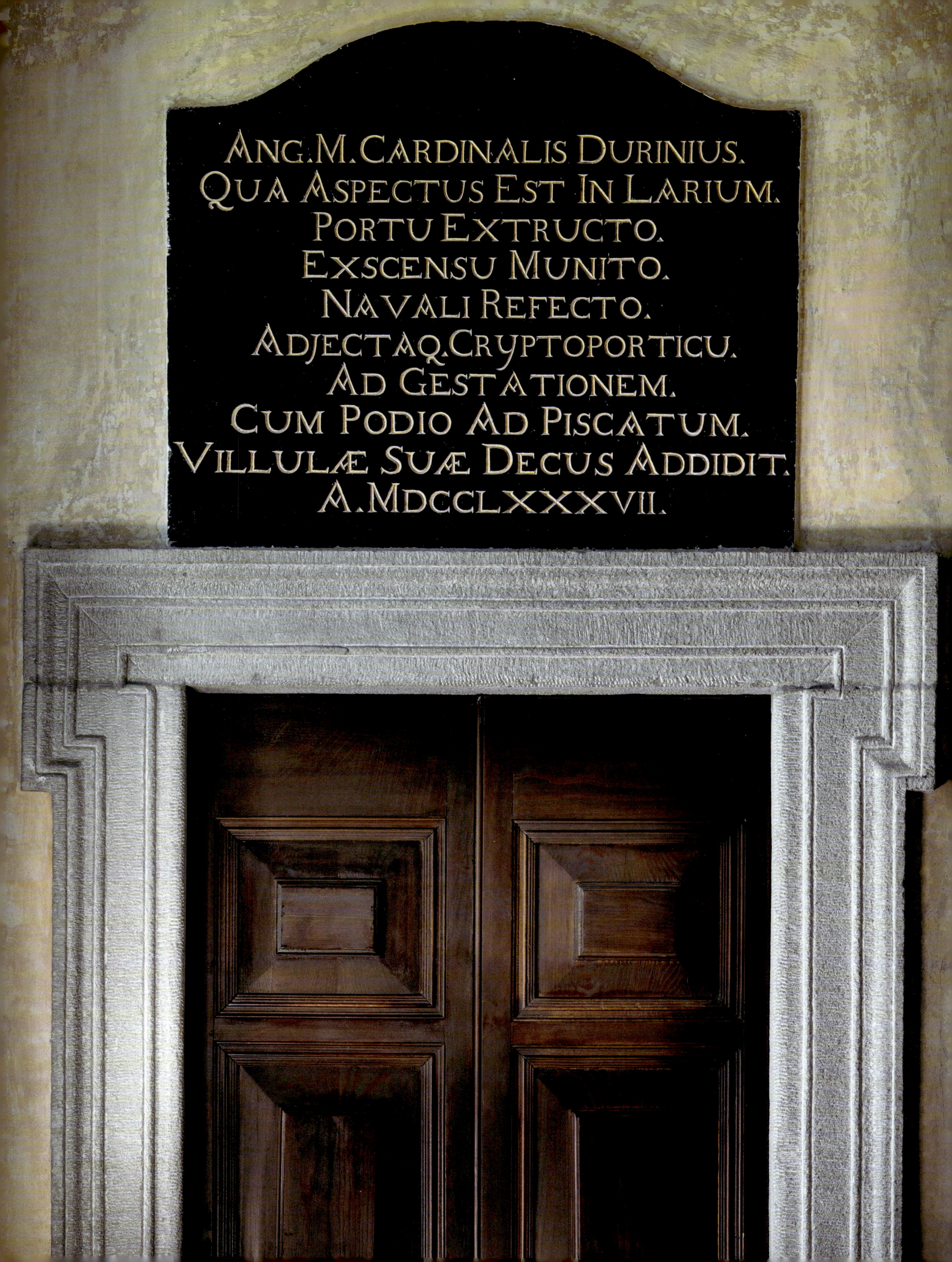
ANG. M. CARDINALIS DURINIUS.
QUA ASPECTUS EST IN LARIUM.
PORTU EXTRUCTO.
EXSCENSU MUNITO.
NAVALI REFECTO.
ADJECTAQ. CRYPTOPORTICU.
AD GESTATIONEM.
CUM PODIO AD PISCATUM.
VILLULÆ SUÆ DECUS ADDIDIT.
A. MDCCLXXXVII.

*"There must be a Lake Como in Paradise,
it being impossible that on earth there is another that
surpasses it in natural beauty. It has thus become,
in a manner of speaking, the place for the entire cultured world...
and now not only noble Lombards but also
Russian dukes, princes, and princesses, Parisian bankers,
and dancers possess a winter palace in Berlin
or St. Petersburg, in Milan or Venice, in London or Paris,
but also a summer villa on Lake Como."*

Johann Georg Kohl, geographer and travel writer, nineteenth century.

PAGES 152–153 The master suite on the second floor is dressed in red. The black wood Régence desk (1720–1725) is attributed to Noël Gérard and stamped "Assnat," which means it was used in the early French national assemblies.
FACING PAGE *Portrait of a Young Nobleman Wearing a Doublet with Sword and Resting his Hand on a Book* by Domenico Tintoretto (1560–1635), son and pupil of Tintoretto (Jacopo Robusti), c. 1600.

TINTORETTO

"The mountains between Como and that village, or rather cluster of villages, are covered on high with chestnut forests… which sometimes descend to the very verge of the lake, overhanging it with their hoary branches. But usually the immediate border of this shore is composed of laurel-trees, and bay, and myrtle, and wild fig-trees, and olives, which grow in the crevices of the rocks, and overhang the caverns, and shadow the deep glens, which are filled with the flashing light of the waterfalls. This shore of the lake is one continued village, and the Milanese nobility have their villas here. The union of culture and the untameable profusion and loveliness of nature is here so close that the line where they are divided can hardly be discovered."

Percy Bysshe Shelley, letter to Thomas Love Peacock, Milan, April 20, 1818.

PAGES 156-157 A Chinese screen composed of twelve Coromandel panels, dating to the first autumn month in the year of Bingchen (1736), encloses the master suite. Courtly figures in a very elaborate landscape are represented on the front. The stool with a gilded wooden frame dates to the Louis XIV period. The seat features shells and bouquets of flowers of rocaille inspiration.
PAGE 158 Detail of one of the two mirrors of the master suite, with a porcelain chinoiserie.
PAGE 159 A baroque carved giltwood stool, covered in floral upholstery. Rome, early eighteenth century.
FACING PAGE Detail of the coffered ceiling in the master suite.

FACING PAGE AND ABOVE Details of a "Fettercairn" bureau in Louis XV style, in kingwood and gilded bronze. At the end of the eighteenth century the bureau belonged to Sir William Forbes (1739–1806), sixth Baronet of Monymusk and Pitsligo (County of Aberdeen) and respected banker, or to one of his descendants having the same name. It is impossible to determine its exact provenance. While its decorations appear Genovese, its materials and neoclassical inspiration are characteristic of Roman cabinetry of that period. The mixture of these two styles produces a completely unique piece.

"The overall impression of the lake is sweet, amorous, Italian.... Everything is surrounded by splendid residences, made for study and for love.... A place where one would like to live and die. A spectacle made to please the eye... all the sentiments of nature are found here together, with the grandiose dominating all."

Gustave Flaubert, *Italie: Notes de voyages*, 1845.

FACING PAGE Sebastiano Conca (1680–1764), *Saint Cecila*, c. 1700. Conca was a painter in the Neapolitan school of Francesco Solimena. The lacquered chest below, finely decorated with gilt and scenes with animals, is of Chinese origin and dates to the late seventeenth century.
PAGES 166–167 The second suite is decorated with a Far Eastern influence, as seen in the lamps made from Imari porcelain vases (early eighteenth century), the small armchair, and the console.

ABOVE Detail of the chest in the second suite.
FACING PAGE Black Chinese Coromandel armchair, mid-eighteenth century, decorated with finely executed and colorful floral details.

PAGES 170–171, ABOVE, AND FACING PAGE A neoclassical Austrian armchair in gilded wood, dating to the late eighteenth century. The Apollo-inspired ornaments and griffins are typical of Austrian furnishings of the period.
PAGES 174–175 Detail of the magnificent Coromandel armoire separating the dressing room and bathroom in the second suite. Far Eastern influences are also found in the bathroom, as well as in the companion, rococo sink console to the one in the master suite.

"The hills sweep upward from the shore,
With villas scattered one by one
Upon their wooded spurs, and lower
Bellaggio blazing in the sun.
And dimly seen, a tangled mass
Of walls and woods, of light and shade,
Stands, beckoning up the Stelvio Pass,
Varenna with its white cascade.
I ask myself, Is this a dream?
Will it all vanish into air?
Is there a land of such supreme
And perfect beauty anywhere?
Sweet vision! Do not fade away;
Linger, until my heart shall take
Into itself the summer day,
And all the beauty of the lake."

Henry Wadsworth Longfellow, "Cadenabbia," 1876–79.

FACING PAGE The double-height music room allows a view from the upper floor from the balcony. Giacomo Durini created this effect by removing the pre-existing ceiling at the beginning of the nineteenth century.
PAGES 178–179 The fireplace in the music room features a sculpted family emblem.
PAGE 180–181 Domenico Tintoretto, *Portrait of Daniel de La Faye*, oil on canvas, c. 1600, and sixteenth-century sculpted emblem on the architrave of the fireplace, representing a lion rampant and a castle.

M.re DANIEL DE LA
FAYE MINISTRE
D'HENRY 4.

ABOVE AND FACING PAGE Large pareclose mirror in carved and gilded wood, attributed to Lorenzo De Ferrari (1680–1744), and detail. An example of early eighteenth-century Genovese rococo, it is similar in style to drawings by Lorenzo De Ferrari for the gilded gallery in Palazzo Carrega-Cataldi in Genoa.
PAGES 184–185 Detail of the mirror, and the cut-glass pendants of the chandelier in the music room.

"It is always springtime with you because your green soil is always in blossom... you are girded by olive groves on both shores... the red of pomegranates shines amidst the lovely gardens... the scent of myrtle berries fills the air... the citron wreathes all with its perfume."

Paulus Diaconus, *Historia Langobardorum*, 786 CE.

FACING PAGE A magnificent late-eighteenth-century Louis XV cut-glass chandelier with brass frame illuminates the music room. The faceted crystal pendants project myriad refractions of light.
PAGE 188 View of the portrait gallery on the third floor balcony.

ABOVE Detail of a door and the floor tiles on the third floor.
The decision was made during the latest restoration to return
to the authentic decorations. Thus Lombard *cotto* tiles
and Bourgogne stone were used to finish the floors in the various rooms.
PAGES 190–191 Full view and detail of a pareclose mirror in carved
and gilded wood. Of mid-eighteenth-century inspiration, it illustrates
the influence of the rocaille in England. The mirror is one of a pair
that was delivered to Ditchley Park, Oxfordshire, standing on the site
of an ancient Roman villa, in the eighteenth century.

IV

A NATURAL REFUGE ON THE LAKESIDE

A NEW SEASON: THE GARDEN

Every garden is a union of nature and architecture: it illustrates the triumph of the human hand over the landscape; it is life transformed into ornament, and, in the best of cases, into art. The designer tries to make this transformation appear natural and spontaneous, but in reality it is a constant and painstaking effort. Changes in taste, fashions, and even economic cycles are all factors that make the garden an eternal work in progress. The garden surrounding Villa Balbiano has witnessed all of this. Its boundaries have changed a number of times over the centuries: crops have given way to geometrical hedges and gravel paths, and buildings have been erected and demolished.

The visitor arriving from the land side beholds a villa set amidst greenery, water, lush vegetation, and open lawns. The wrought-iron entrance gate leads into an oval enclosure, where a fountain splashes water onto an aquatic garden of lily pads floating in a geometrical pool. From there, twin gravel paths border a lawn with a stepped watercourse in the centre and lead down to the entrance to the villa, which is majestically flanked by cypresses on either side. The high evergreen oak hedges (*Quercus ilex*) on either side of the promenade are punctuated with arched openings and statues, like a symmetrical pair of theatre loges. The composition of the landscape has been refined over the centuries: the oval entrance with its fountain is documented to the eighteenth century, and the other elements were added in the nineteenth and twentieth.

As the villa was being restored to its current state, it also made sense to rework the immediate space around it. This involved reuniting plots of land that had been separated, seeking to foster harmony and unity throughout. The British landscape architecture firm Colson Stone Practice, who had also advised on the gardens at Villa Astor in Sorrento, was commissioned for this task.

The first step was to compile a list of the trees and shrubs that were in a poor state of health and undertake historical research to understand how the property had evolved over time. Land registry maps, paintings, photographs, and satellite images were all used to reconstruct the villa's complex history. This phase took about six months. Meetings and discussions with the owners played a particularly important role in re-envisioning the soul of the garden.

The replanting took just over a year. One of the first decisions was to thin out the area on the west side, between the villa and the lake, where the outdoor swimming pool is now. At the time it was very densely planted with trees and other vegetation. A group of sweet olives (*Osmanthus fragrans*) had grown out of control and now reached the height of the third-floor windows. From the grand salons on the second floor, one looked out into a thicket of branches, making the rooms dark and oppressive. The decision was made not to remove the trees, but to prune them back and give them time to adapt to a new form. This opened up vistas between the villa and the lake and allowed the evening sun to illuminate the building and the swimming pool, itself now in the midst of a large lawn artfully planted with Maindenhair trees (*Ginkgo biloba*), a Japanese pagoda tree (*Sophora japonica*), and a number of copper beeches (*Fagus sylvatica purpurea*).

While the building traces its origins to the sixteenth century, the Italian-style garden is much more recent, dating to the 1960s. The central fountain, with the water cascading down in steps toward the villa, as well as the high linear hedges date to that period. Little was done to alter the historical arrangement and spaces in the garden, although all that remains as evidence of its earlier layout is the old stone arch in the rose garden. Once part of an enclosure wall, it is now a decorative architectural element amidst the greenery. The geometry of the garden harmonizes with the rectangular villa and creates a stunning line of sight up to the entrance gate. This perspective is amplified by other transversal views uniting statues and other decorative elements. The scenery, changing by hour and by season, is a never-ending source of wonder for visitors.

The landscape designers collaborated closely with the architects working on the villa and there is a very clear and strong relationship between the interior of the villa and the outdoor space that surrounds it; they are both united in one great composition. The new layout with its large flower beds testifies to the owners' desire for a more ornamental garden. Some six thousand five hundred new plants were added to the existing vegetation, including different varieties of roses and other species that are unusual for the area, adding a touch of unique charm to the property. The framework of the garden is composed entirely of evergreens, and thus maintains its identity year-round. However, the owners specifically requested that the garden bloom for the longest period possible and so the first flowers open in the early spring and the last in September and October. In November the vegetation becomes pure architecture until spring.

PAGES 194–195 The path to the villa seen from the second-floor window. The high evergreen oak and bay laurel hedges guide the visitor from the gate to the front door.
ABOVE Detail of the wrought-iron gate, which gives visitors their first view of Villa Balbiano.
PAGES 198–199 The grand main entrance with its double exedra vestibule.

The flowering plants are a mix of shrubs, herbaceous perennials, and trees reflecting British taste to some extent, but incorporated into the structure of a typical Italian garden. Windmill palms (*Trachycarpus fortunei*), Japanese laurels (*Aucuba japonica*), dwarf oleanders (*Nerium oleander 'Nana'*), soft shield-ferns (*Polystichum setiferum*), sedum 'Autumn Joy' (*Sedum Herbstfreude*), Easter lily (*Lilium longiflorum*), and oakleaf hydrangea (*Hydrangea quercifolia*), just to name a few, enhance this picturesque scene.

Near the villa there is a vegetable garden as well as a fruit orchard. Apples, pears, and figs are planted along the enclosure wall or trained on trellises to create a covered pergola walk. The original vegetable garden was expanded at the owners' request. And, as was the case with the work to restore the villa, the redesign of the garden required close collaboration with the Superintendency. The entire scheme had to be approved and specific permits issued, for example, to allow the cutting of trees (even if they were diseased or dead), or to remove a part of the garden wall, even though it had been a relatively recent addition.

Thanks to the meticulous attention to detail, beautiful finish, and a sensitive interpretation of the historical context, in 2017 the project won first prize for the best restoration of an historic garden from the prestigious British Society of Garden Designers.

The garden is now thriving, producing flowers and fruits, and water can be heard gurgling in the fountain once again. Villa Balbiano has been restored to its historic magnificence, and its charm endures across the centuries, beautifully reflected in the waters of Lake Como. ◆

ABOVE View from the garden of the mountains beyond the lake. The villa is framed by monumental cypress trees.
FACING PAGE The pool with its rich carpet of water lilies occupies the center of an oval created in the seventeenth century. The owners made sure it was preserved and restored, along with the fountain in the center, created in the eighteenth century.

ABOVE AND FACING PAGE The gardens of Villa Balbiano are filled with decorative touches. Urns and statues nestle into their green setting.
PAGES 204-205 The high hedges have regularly spaced arched openings that reveal statues and make it possible to circulate freely through the garden.

FACING PAGE AND PAGES 208–209 Detail of a statue nestling among vegetation.
ABOVE Italian statues in white marble from the second half of the nineteenth century representing Hebe—the Greek personification of eternal youth, known as Juventas to the Romans—following the models of Antonio Canova (1757–1822) on the left, and Bertel Thorvaldsen (1770–1844) on the right.

ABOVE AND FACING PAGE The urns and busts dotting the garden were brought here between the eighteenth and the twentieth centuries.
PAGE 212–213 Detail of one of the statues in white Carrara marble, dating from the second half of the nineteenth century, and representing Hebe, after a model by Bertel Thorvaldsen, and a decorative element of the garden.

"High mountains rise behind, their lower terraces bearing olives, vines, and Indian corn; midway clothed by chestnut woods; bare, rugged, sublime, at their summits. The waters of the lake are spread before; the villa-studded promontory of Bellagio being immediately opposite, and further off the shores of the other branch of the lake, with the town of Varenna, sheltered by gigantic mountains. Highest among them is the Resegone, so frequently mentioned by Manzoni in the Promessi Sposi, *with its summit jagged like a saw. Indeed, all these Alps are in shape more abrupt and fantastic than any I ever saw."*

Mary Shelley, *Rambles in Germany and Italy in 1840, 1842, and 1843*, 1844.

FACING PAGE The veranda provides a quiet place for visitors to enjoy the changing landscape over the course of the day.
PAGES 218-219 Framed by evergreens, the garden preserves its allure all year round.

"Down below were the gardens, bare now
but beautifully regular, the gravel paths, the trees,
the stone wall by the lake and the lake
in the sunlight with the mountains beyond.
I stood at the window looking out."

Ernest Hemingway, *A Farewell to Arms*, 1929.

PAGES 220-221 The design of the garden, architecture, and measured decoration testifies to the owners' desire to preserve the harmony and unity that reign on the lake.
FACING PAGE Hidden by vegetation and simply marked by a wrought-iron gate, the boathouse can only be seen from the lake.
PAGES 224-225 One of the best ways to experience lake Como is from the water. This traditional dock provides access to the lake from the green oasis of the garden.

"Awaiting the ferry
We watch the setting sun
Drench the lakeside town
And the lake itself
In golden light
As if to remind us
That we need not seek elsewhere:
Immanence is the mystery"

Charles Tomlinson, "Varenna," 1993.

FACING PAGE Detail of a Lime tree (*Tilia cordata*) embellishing the lush garden. PAGES 228-229 Sunset view of the mountains surrounding Lake Como.

FACING PAGE AND ABOVE At nightfall, the many chandeliers in the villa decorate the façade with light. On a still evening, the outdoor pool becomes a mirror reflecting the sky.

"Sleeps the lake; white-branched beeches
Bend twisted limbs above
Interweaving mirrored shadows
In its quiet dark depths.
Tremble, whisper white-branched beeches;
And it, still-standing, does not even flinch. . . .
Sometimes only its surfaces
Are startled by a shed-leaf-trace."

Pencho Slavejkov, "A Dream for Happiness," 1958.

FACING PAGE The placid waters of Lake Como invite you to discover villas along the shore and small, colorful villages nestled between water and mountains.
PAGES 234-235 The glassed-in archways on either side of the indoor pool provide beautiful views of the garden and the lake.
PAGES 236-237 The patio mixes the warm color of stone with the pale violet of wisteria, creating a natural outdoor extension of the villa.

INDEX

Page numbers in *italics* correspond to captions, page numbers in **bold** correspond to quotations.

FACING PAGE Cypresses framing the villa.
PAGES 240-241 Comacina Island, the only island in Lake Como, lies a few hundred yards from the shore within clear sight of Villa Balbiano.

ACKNOWLEDGMENTS

The author wishes to thank Suzanne Tise-Isoré, editorial director of the Style & Design collection at Flammarion, and her team—Bernard Lagacé, Lysandre Le Cléac'h, Lara Lo Calzo, and Gwendoline Blanchard—for their unfailing support throughout the project; Bruno Ehrs for his remarkable photographs capturing the full majesty of Villa Balbiano; Alain Blaustein for the beautiful images of villas on Lake Como; and Andrew Zega and Bernd H. Dams for their gorgeous watercolors. He also wishes to express his gratitude to Jacques Garcia, Carlota Proença de Almeida, Christian Sweet of Colston Stone Practice, and John Dineen of Quercia Private Ltd for the fruitful exchanges during work on this publication. A very special thanks goes to scholar Luca M. Visconti for his valuable support and suggestions; to Mauro Livraga, of Superintendence of Archives for the Lombardy Regional Government, who provided the fascinating stories contained within a notarial document or an inventory; to Daniele Marucci and the staff of the Sormani Library of Milan for their generous support; to Madame Rita Ajmone-Cat for her generosity; and to Cristina Geddo, Cristian Copes, and Guido Scaramellini whose impressive research, published in works of great historical importance, provided an indispensable starting point for this book.

BIBLIOGRAPHY

ALBERTONI, Ettore Adalberto, cur. *I magistri comacini nella storia e per lo sviluppo del Lago di Como e della Valle d'Intelvi*. Milan: Libri Scheiwiller, 2006.

BERTOLOTTI, Davide. *Viaggio al lago di Como*. C.A. Ostinelli, 1821.

CANI, Fabio. *La Pliniana di Torno: storia di una villa e di un mito sul lago di Como*. Como: Alessandro Dominioni Editore, 2010.

CANI, Fabio and Gerardo Monizza. *Como e la sua storia: dalla preistoria all'attualità*. Como: NodoLibri, 1999.

COPES, Cristian and Guido Scaramellini. *Il Balbiano: un palazzo a Ossuccio. Una dimora dei Gallio sul lago di Como sorta su magnifiche rovine cinquecentesche*. Como: Enzo Pifferi Editore, 2012.

COSTANZA FATTORI, Lionello. "Architetture neoclassiche nel territorio comasco." *Arte lombarda*. Milan: Vita e Pensiero, 1980.

DETTAMANTI, Pietro. *Viaggio al lago di Como: letterati e viaggiatori dell'Ottocento sul Lario* (vol. 78). Moncalieri (TO): C.I.R.V.I., 2007.

Fondo Acchiappati – inventario d'archivio. City of Como historical archives, 2002.

GEDDO, Cristina, ed. *Omaggio al cardinale Angelo Maria Durini, mecenate di lettere ed arti*. Papers from the conference at the Biblioteca Braidense, Milan, January 26, 2012. Contributions by C. Capra, C. Geddo, S. Graciotti, F. Milani, M. Natale, and W. Spaggiari. Novara: Poligrafica moderna, 2013.

GIOVIO, Paolo. *La descrizione del Lario* (first edition: 1537). Milan: Edizioni Il Polifilo, 2007.

GROS, Pierre et Mario Torelli. *Storia dell'urbanistica. Il mondo romano*. Rome: Editori Laterza, 2007.

LURASCHI, Giorgio. *Storia di Como antica*. Cermenate (CO): New Press Edizioni, 1997.

PERON, Ettore Maria. *Storia di Como dalle origini ai giorni nostri*. Pordenone: Edizioni Biblioteca dell'Immagine, 2017.

PIFFERI, Enzo and Giuseppe Rasi. *Ville e giardini del lago di Como*. Como: Enzo Pifferi Editore, 2005.

PREVITERA, Maria Angela, Serena Bertolucci, and Maria Fratelli. *Novecento sul lago di Como. Pittura tra acque e monti*. Milan: Editore Nexo, 2013.

RIZZINI, Marialuisa. "Note sul collezionismo seicentesco: la famiglia Gallio di Como," *Arte Lombarda*. Milan: Vita e Pensiero, 1991.

ZIMMERMANN, T. C. *Paolo Giovio. Uno storico e la crisi italiana del XVI secolo*. Milan: Lampi di Stampa, 2012.

PHOTOGRAPHIC CREDITS

All photographs in this book were taken by Bruno Ehrs except for those on the following pages:
22: © Granger/Bridgeman Images; 23: © RMN-Grand Palais (domaine de Chantilly)/Michel Urtado; 24: © Beaux-Arts de Paris, Dist. RMN-Grand Palais/image INHA; 25: © Daniele Marucci; 26: © RMN-Grand Palais/Michel Urtado; 28–29: © Bibliothèque nationale de France; 30: © Beaux-Arts de Paris, Dist. RMN-Grand Palais/image INHA; 31: © akg-images/MPortfolio/Electa; 32: © BPK, Berlin, Dist. RMN-Grand Palais/image BStGS; 33: © De Agostini Picture Library/Scala, Florence; 34–35: © De Agostini/Leemage; overlay: Bibliothèque nationale de France. 37: © Alan Blaustein Photography; 40: Alan Blaustein Photography; 41: De Agostini Picture Library/Age Fotostock; 42: © De Agostini/Ambrosiana/Leemage; 43: © Musei Civici di Como; 44: © Château de Versailles, Dist. RMN-Grand Palais/image château de Versailles; 49, 50: © De Agostini/Leemage; 51: © Tate, London, Dist. RMN-Grand Palais/Tate Photography; 52–53: © British Library Board. All Rights Reserved/Bridgeman Images; 54: © De Agostini/Getty Images; 55: © Suzanne Tise-Isoré, 2018; 56–57: © Archivi Alinari, Firenze; 58: © Musei Civici Monza; 60l: © Private Collection/Mondadori Portfolio/Electa/Sergio Anelli/Bridgeman Images; 60r: © Copper engraving by Piotti from drawing by Andrea Appiani/De Agostini/Galleria Garisenda/Bridgeman Images; 61: © Camera di Commercio Como/photos Daniele Marucci; 62: Ms. 2657, f. 24v © Bibliothèque municipale d'Avignon/photo IRHT; 63: © Private collection; 69–73: © Alan Blaustein Photography; 75–77: © Andrew Zega and Bernd H. Dams, 2018; 89: © Bernard Lagacé, 2018; 200: © Suzanne Tise-Isoré, 2018; 231: © Bernard Lagacé, 2018; 246: © Suzanne Tise-Isoré, 2018.
Every effort has been made to identify photographers and copyright holders of the images reproduced in this book.
Any errors or omissions referred to the Publisher will be corrected in subsequent printings.

FACING PAGE Bell tower of the church of Santa Maria Maddalena in Ossuccio.
PAGES 244-245 The architecture of the vehicle entrance to Villa Balbiano on the village side, and the footbridge over the Perlana River.

ABOVE The Roman-inspired bust of Alexander the Great stands in a corner of the stairway.
ENDPAPERS A bucolic view of Lake Como in the eighteenth century, in a detail from the painting decorating the walls of the indoor pool room.

EXECUTIVE DIRECTOR
Suzanne Tise-Isoré
Style & Design Collection

EDITORIAL COORDINATION
Lara Lo Calzo

GRAPHIC DESIGN
Bernard Lagacé
assisted by Lysandre Le Cléac'h

TRANSLATED FROM ITALIAN BY
Language Consulting Congressi, Milan

COPYEDITING AND PROOFREADING
Lindsay Porter

PRODUCTION
Élodie Conjat

COLOR SEPARATION
Les Artisans du Regard, Paris

PRINTED BY
Musumeci, Italy

Simultaneously published in French as *Villa Balbiano, Splendeurs italiennes sur le lac de Côme.*

Flammarion S.A.
87, quai Panhard-et-Levassor
75647 Paris Cedex 13
editions.flammarion.com
styleetdesign-flammarion.com

18 19 20 3 2 1
ISBN: 978-2-08-020365-6
Legal Deposit: May 2018